Contents

KT-524-939

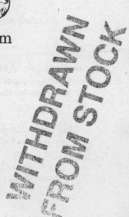

Foul Football

EVEN FOULER FOOTBALL

MICHAEL COLEMAN

www.michael-coleman.com

*Illustrated by
Mike Phillips*

Hippo

For Mike 'phantastic' Phillips
also Helen, Ali, Jill and Susila

Scholastic Children's Books,
Commonwealth House, 1–19 New Oxford Street,
London WC1A 1NU, UK
A division of Scholastic Ltd
London ~ New York ~ Toronto ~ Sydney ~ Auckland
Mexico City ~ New Delhi ~ Hong Kong

Published in the UK by Scholastic Ltd, 2004

ISBN 0 439 97748 7

INTRODUCTION

Football is the most popular sport in the world. It began in England (say the English)...

From its birth in England (if you believe the English), football has grown so much that it's now the most popular, most-played game in the world. At this minute, right now, somewhere in the world, a footballer will be scoring a goal or making a save – or committing a foul!

Yes (as the first book in this series, *Foul Football*, revealed), although the game the English invented (if you believe them) is a beautiful game it can also be pretty foul. But is it the same everywhere? Do other countries have a similar share of foul football? Is it less foul than in the place where it all began (if you believe the English). Or is it a case of foreign football being even fouler football?

This is the book to help you decide! It's got everything you need to make up your mind about where football's foulest. For instance, super stories about football folk like...

- The kindly English referee who took pity on the losing team.
- The Brazilian coach who got angry if his team didn't foul enough.

- The even fouler Uruguayan player found guilty of daylight robbery.

And, because football is about more than people, it's got a host of foul facts you need to bear in mind too, like those about...

- The foul South American crash helmet which stopped a match.
- The world competition which was better known for its foul fights than its football.

And you can weigh these against even fouler facts like this one about...

- The English ground which tried to swallow a footballer.

Plus, to provide even more help in your decision-making, we'll be handing out our coveted *Foul Football* awards. They'll only be presented to a select few, to those who've either done something really beautiful – or something even fouler than usual. Awards such as...

THE PITCH RAGE AWARD...

Ataulfo Valencia of Ecuadorian club Espoli, who was sent off a minute before the end of a South American cup tie against Ecuador's Barcelona. Why? Did he commit a foul foul? No. Did Ataulfo retaliate after being 'acked? No. A trolley being used to ferry an injured player off the pitch accidentally bumped into him. Violent Valencia got a red card (and wins his even fouler award) because instead of seeing the funny side he jumped up and punched the driver!

So read on. And whatever you do, don't make up your mind before you reach the last page. That wouldn't be fair!

FOOTBALL FAR AND WIDE

Let's start by looking at how football (foul or fair) came to be played throughout the world. Did each country invent its own version? Or was the game carried to foreign shores by visitors, like a (nice) kind of football 'flu? In particular, did the game begin in England or is that a foul football fib?

Enterprising England

Let's set the facts straight. When the English say that nobody had ever played a game anything like football until they did, they're wrong. Not telling foul football fibs, just wrong. Football-like games had been played in lots of places before the English tried it. A sport similar to football was played 3,000 years ago in Japan, and Chinese writing from over 1,800 years ago talks about a football-type game played between teams from Japan and China. That's right, international matches! The game was called *Tsu Chu* which translated means football – Tsu means to kick with the foot and Chu means a ball made of leather and stuffed.

The ancient Greeks and Romans also played a game that was a bit like football – although the Greeks' version was closer to rugby because players were allowed to carry the ball. There were even organized matches in ancient Rome – with 27 men on each side!

I HATE THESE DEFENSIVE WALLS!

So, football probably wasn't invented in England. But nobody can deny that what the enterprising English *did* do was to get things organized. They turned a general rough-house sport into a game with a set of rules and, in 1863, formed their own Football Association (FA) – the first in the world.

These rules were then carried across the world. Sailors and teachers and railwaymen carried them from England to countries in which they'd found work. Visitors to England heard about the rules and took them back home with them. Maybe that's why the English sing a song called: 'Rule Britannia!'

THESE NEW RULE BOOKS ARE REALLY USEFUL!

SORRY!

Korean kicks and Japanese jinks

In 2002, the World Cup finals were jointly held in South Korea and Japan, the first time they'd been played in Asia. And about time too, the Koreans and Japanese must have thought (although they were far too polite to say so).

As we've already seen, a football-like game was played in Japan 3,000 years ago. But the Koreans weren't new boys either. Korean history books tell of a football-like game called "chuk-kook" being played there well over 1,000 years ago!

Even the modern game had been known in Korea for well over 100 years. In 1882 the crew of a British ship called *Flying Fish* arrived in the port of Jemulpo, Incheon. Whenever the sailors came ashore they brought a football with them for a kick-about. The local lads soon joined in the fun – making such good friends with the sailors that when their ship set sail they left their football behind as a gift.

Slowly, the popularity of football grew in Korea and in 1904 it was given another big boost. This time it wasn't due to a group of sailors – but to a bunch of teachers. Deciding that their students needed something more energetic to study than maths and science, Korea's Royal Foreign Language School added football to the list of class subjects.

By the 1920s the first Korean football league had been formed. Korea was divided into north and south in 1945. In 1948, South Korea's international team competed in the London Olympic Games, and from 1956–60 the country were the undisputed Asian champions. In 1983, the South Koreans established the first professional league in Asia (it currently has 10 teams). North Korea weren't doing too badly either; they reached the World Cup quarter finals in 1966. Sounds like the teachers did a good job!

The arrival of modern football in Japan was confusing, to say the least. The game officially reached the country in 1873, when a game was organized at the Naval Academy in Tokyo by a British officer, Archibald Douglas, and his men. The trouble was that many of the Japanese spectators thought the match was a version of *kemari*, an ancient Japanese ball game connected with the Shinto religion!

Although the game became more popular (once people realized it *was* a game!) the Japanese Football Association wasn't formed until 1921 – and only then because something unexpected arrived to persuade them. An all-Japan Schools Soccer Tournament had just been started and the English FA had generously sent a replica of the famous FA Cup to be used as the trophy. This was something of an embarrassment because Japan didn't have a Football Association to officially receive such a splendid gift. They had to form one just for the purpose!

The following year, an amateur Japan Soccer League was established, with eight teams. Japan's football stayed strictly amateur until 1993, when the professional J-league began with such stars as England striker Gary Lineker. He's no longer playing, but the J-league is still going strong!

Born in Brazil

In 2002, Brazil became the world football champions for a record fifth time – but who can claim the credit for introducing the Brazilians to the game? There are lots of different stories. Some say it was due to British and Dutch sailors playing football matches on the beach while their ships were in port. Another gives the credit to a couple of Englishmen, named John and Hugh, who are supposed to have taught the game to the railway workers they employed.

The only story with real evidence to back it up, though, concerns a man with the very un-Brazilian name Charles Miller. This was because, although he was born in Brazil, his parents were English. It also explains why a not-very-cheerful Charlie was packed off to school in England. He was a lot happier when he came back, though, in 1894. He'd discovered football! Now aged 20, Miller brought with him loads of football gear and a wild enthusiasm to tell everybody about the great game he'd discovered. He did, too. Only eight years later the São Paulo league was formed. Brazil were on their way to glory!

By 1914 they had an international team. Starting the way they meant to carry on, Brazil's first-ever "international" match was a 2–1 win in a friendly match against English club side Exeter City. One of their goals that day was scored by another Brazilian with a very un-Brazilian name: Artur Friedenreich.

Friedenreich was the first great Brazilian striker. Born in 1892, he had a German father and a Brazilian mother, which qualified him to play for Brazil. After notching up that goal against Exeter, awesome Artur went on scoring for the next 20 years! Nicknamed "The Tiger", fearsome Friedenreich became the first player in the world to notch up 1,000 goals. By the time his career finally ended he'd banged in a grand total of 1,329!

Nifty Nigeria

Englishmen may or may not have carried their football rules to Africa, but the English influence can be seen in that continent, too. Nigeria, for example, didn't form a national football association until 1945. When they did, what was their first move? To establish their own version of the FA Cup!

Just like the English version, it began in a small way with just nine teams, all from the capital city, Lagos. Gradually other teams joined until, in 1953, a team named Kano became the first from outside Lagos to win the cup.

There have been record wins, too. Just as Preston's 26–0 beating of Hyde is still an English FA Cup record, so the Nigerian version is Warri's 18–0 whacking of Igala. Desperate losers are there, too. Between 1963 and 1974, poor Plateau were losing finalists eight times!

Of course in England nothing stops the FA Cup from taking place. But in 1973, the Nigerian FA Cup wasn't held at all so as to allow the country to concentrate on hosting the second All-Africa Games. Then there was the 1977 Cup Final, which started but didn't finish. Already 1–0 down and complaining about biased refereeing, Raccah Rovers refused to come out for the second half of their game against IICC Shooting Stars!

Nowadays Nigeria and the other African nations are steadily catching up with the rest of the footballing world. Will an African nation lift the World Cup one day? Don't bet against it. In the 1996 Olympic Games, Nigeria beat Brazil 4–3 in the semi-final. Not content with that, they went on to beat Argentina 3–2 in the final to become the first African nation to win the gold medal.

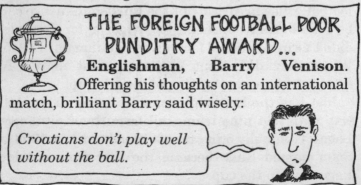

THE FOREIGN FOOTBALL POOR PUNDITRY AWARD...

Englishman, Barry Venison. Offering his thoughts on an international match, brilliant Barry said wisely:

Croatians don't play well without the ball.

The league-of-their-own quiz

The English flair for organization didn't only give football its rules, it produced ideas for organized competitions, too. Every knock-out competition in the world is based on an English invention, the FA Cup. The same goes for league competitions. The English Football League led the way in 1887–88, and soon other countries began to follow. Now, every football country has a league competition.

Here are just ten of the hundreds of leagues being played today. Match the names of each league against its host country.

LEAGUE NAME

① PREMIERSHIP (THE FIRST IN THE WORLD).
② BUNDESLIGA
③ K-LEAGUE
④ CAMPEONATO
⑤ LA LIGA
⑥ CHAMPIONNAT
⑦ APERTURA
⑧ SERIE
⑨ J-LEAGUE
⑩ SUPERETTAN

COUNTRY

ⓐ KOREA
ⓑ ITALY
ⓒ BRAZIL
ⓓ FRANCE
ⓔ SCOTLAND
ⓕ SWEDEN
ⓖ JAPAN
ⓗ ARGENTINA
ⓘ GERMANY
ⓙ SPAIN

Answers:
1e) Scotland formed a Premier Division in 1975, 17 years before the English! 2i) 3a) The K-League is played from spring to late autumn. 4c) 5j) 6d) 7h) 8b) 9g) It began in 1993. 10f)

17

Top of the world

Since 1993, every football-playing country in the world has been playing in a kind of league. Not a proper league, where each team plays every other, but a pretend league. It's called The FIFA/Coca-Cola World Ranking – because it's controlled by the world-governing body, FIFA, using sponsorship (and a huge computer program) provided by the drinks company.

The idea of the league table is to show how good (or bad) any country is at football. You could try and do the same sort of thing for the school teams in your area – if you're brave. Here's a rough idea of how you'd score ranking points whenever you play a match:

● By winning or drawing the game.

● By losing the game! Put up a good show against Manchester Marvels, a team ranked higher than you, and you earn bonus points. On the other hand, beating Walsall Wobblers, a weaker team than you, won't earn you many points.

● By scoring goals. Same thing again – a goal scored against a strong team like Rochdale Rock-hards counts more than one strolled in against Sunderland Sponges. Also the first goal scored is worth more than any others!

● By not letting in goals. Let in a goal and points are taken away. Concede a goal to lowly ranked Useless United and a lot of points are deducted.

● By being the away team. The away team earns a little bonus for having to cope with the greater number of mums, dads and teachers shouting for the home team.

- By playing important matches. Winning a friendly kick-about behind the bike sheds counts for less than lifting the cup at a big-time, inter-schools final.
- By living where you do. The points your team scores are adjusted depending on whether the teams in your area are generally strong or generally weak.

THE TEAMS IN OUR AREA ARE GENERALLY WEAK.

- By learning how to count up to seven. Playing a hundred games in a season won't necessarily help your team shoot up to the top of the ranking list. Only your seven best-scoring games count, however many you play.
- By trying hard year after year. The points you score in a season are mixed in with the points you've scored in the previous seven seasons. So if your team once luckily beat Liverpool Legends when all their players were away from school with measles, then that historic victory will help your ranking for a while.

Phew!

Moving, moving, moving

In the real FIFA rankings, each year there are two awards:

- The "Team of the Year" award goes to the team scoring the most points from their seven qualifying matches.
- The "Best Mover of the Year" award goes to the team which comes out on top after an even fouler bit of arithmetic – multiplying the points each team had at the start of the year by the points they earned during the year. This is supposed to give teams already high in the ranking the chance to win an award. (Get your teacher to prove that it does – or, if you want to be sure of getting the sums right, check it out for yourself!)

Here are five international teams. Put them in the order you think they finished in the "Best Mover" table at the end of World Cup year 2002.

Rock bottom

Which teams get the foulest headaches when they see they're propping up the rest in the rankings list? The lowest team in Europe is the world's oldest and smallest independent republic, San Marino. Not surprising really, there are only 1,200 players in the whole country! They haven't won many international matches – but then they don't expect to. As one of their coaches, Giampaolo Mazza, said:

Our aim isn't always to win, but to give the best possible account of ourselves while defending our nation's colours.

Even so, in September 2003, San Marino were ranked in 158th position, a long way from the bottom of the 204-country table.

21

So who were officially the worst team in the world? Here, in alphabetical order, are the bottom five. Sort them into their descending order of dismalness!

AMERICAN SAMOA:
GUAM:
MONTSERRAT:
PUERTO RICO:
TURKS AND CAICOS ILANDS:

Answer:

Puerto Rico were in 200th place; 201st were Guam; 202nd American Samoa; 203rd were Turks and Caicos Islands; in 204th position and officially the worst international country in the world – the Caribbean island of Montserrat.

Still, don't judge Montserrat too harshly. In 1995 a large lump of the island disappeared when a volcano erupted! Not surprisingly, football on the island came to a halt – how would your team cope if its pitch and training facilities disappeared for ever under a heap of molten lava? The Montserratians are made of tough stuff, though. A five-team league restarted in 2000 and improving their world ranking is their next target. Well, at least it can't get any worse!

CLUB COMPENDIUM

Every football-playing country has its big clubs whose names are known all over the world. Never forget, though that every big club was once a little club with an urge to grow.

In England, for example, you can bet that when the Newton Heath (Lancashire and Yorkshire Railway) Football Club was formed in 1878, at least one of its founders would lie in bed every night dreaming that their team would one day grow into a world-famous team called – oh, Manchester United, say. (Which they did!)

Likewise you can be sure that when a group of bomb-making workers got together in 1886 and called their team Dial Square FC, at least one of them hoped that they'd explode into a league and cup double-winning side with a name like – say, Arsenal. (Which they did!)

Here's a grower's guide to how some of the world's top club sides began.

I've had this great idea...

Ajax (Holland)

Dutch enthusiast Han Dade was the owner of what, in 1883, was a rare article – a real leather football! Not surprisingly, he was popular with his mates. So when Han suggested they form a football club in 1900 he wasn't short of players – at least, not until Han's rules began to bite. Determined Dade ensured that Ajax club members played fair not foul by ruling that they could be fined for such things as:

- not telling the captain they were going to be absent
- "inappropriate words or acts" (that is, foul language or foul play)
- not paying attention.

ARE YOU PAYING ATTENTION?

ER?

The players obviously said "fair enough", because Ajax went on to become not only the most famous team in Holland, but also the team with the reputation for being the fairest.

Barcelona (Spain)

Who says footballers only look at the pictures in the newspapers? If the residents of Barcelona hadn't been able to read, their club might never have been formed. That's because the way Swiss businessman Hans Gamper set about finding players for a new team was to put an advert in a local sports magazine. This was on 22 October 1899, and just one month later a meeting was held to set up the club – with an English president, Gualteri Wild. Three years later Barcelona reached the Spanish Cup final.

Bayern Munich (Germany)

Another man with an English name gets the credit for setting up the top German club. Franz John already played for a club called MTV 1879 but he wasn't happy. On 27 February 1900, John called a meeting of other miserable MTV-men at a restaurant. During their meal, the gathering carved out plans to set up a new club called FC Bayern. Their move certainly served up a nasty surprise for their old club, MTV. Bayern's first match was against Franz John's former team and they ran out 7–1 winners!

Boca Juniors (Argentina)

Pat MacCarthy left his native Ireland on a ship, which ended up in the Argentine port of La Boca, in Buenos Aires. He found he wasn't alone. He was surrounded not only by fellow Irish immigrants, but by Italians as well, all looking for work. It wasn't long before they were soon labouring side by side, loading and unloading ships, but they didn't speak the same language – at least, not until they all began kicking a football around during their rest periods. Then they understood each other! In 1905, the work-mates formed Boca Juniors FC, and the club has been supported as "the team of the workers" ever since.

Glasgow Celtic (Scotland)

Celtic were formed in 1887 thanks to another Irishman, by the name of Walfrid. But was "Walfrid" **a)** his first name, or **b)** his second name?

In the nineteenth-century, Scotland was the destination for thousands of Irish immigrants forced by famine to leave their homeland to try and find work in Glasgow's factories and shipyards. Unfortunately there simply weren't enough jobs to go round, so Brother Walfrid had the idea of starting a football club. He thought it would give his poor parishioners in the Parkhead area an interest

On 28 May 1888, Celtic played their first game. A crowd of 2,000 turned up to see them win 5–2 in a friendly against a team from the other end of the city. Their name? Rangers.

THE IT'S-ONLY-FAIR-TO-LET-HIM-IN-FOR-NOTHING AWARD...

Brother Walfrid. In recognition of the part he played in setting up the club, Brother Walfrid (and any other Catholic priest) was allowed in to watch Celtic's home matches free – a tradition that was maintained for over 100 years.

Dynamo Kiev (Ukraine)

In terms of age, Dynamo Kiev are youngsters. They weren't founded until 1927. At the time, Ukraine was part of the Soviet Union and the usual thing was for sports teams to represent the organizations that their players worked for – which is how Dynamo Kiev came into being. The Soviet Union was a massive country with an equally massive police force to keep foul behaviour under control – and Dynamo were their team. Yes, the Kiev kickers wore police boots for work and football boots for play!

AC Milan (Italy)

For a top Italian football club, AC Milan was founded in a curious way. Three Englishmen (not Italian men) decided over a glass of beer (not wine) to form a ... cricket (not football) club!

This happened in December 1899 when – believe it or not – cricket was much more popular than football. The members' aim for the Milan Cricket and Football Club was to play cricket as much as possible and try to encourage others to take up football.

They succeeded! You'd have to look very hard to find any cricket balls at a Milan match nowadays.

Panathanaikos (Greece)

This top Greek team had no need to look for either a doctor or a trainer after they were formed (as the Athens Football Club) by George Calafatis in 1908. Clever Calafatis could cope with both fouls and fitness because he'd studied medicine at the University of Athens and gymnastics at the Academy of Gymnastics. He was talented enough to have been an Olympic athlete but his great love was football. He wasn't bad at that, either. His team's first official match was a 9–0 victory, with goal-grabber George hitting a hat trick!

Penarol (Uruguay)

Not every club has been *totally* grateful to its founders – but in Penarol's case it's understandable. Formed by workers at the British-owned Central Uruguayan Railway company in 1891, they started life with the mouthful of a name:

CENTRAL URUGUAYAN RAILWAY CRICKET CLUB

But by 1913 two things had happened. Football fanaticism had taken hold, and the British had begun to leave the country to work elsewhere. The Central Uruguayan Railway was handed over to the Uruguayans. As fast as a flying winger the club changed its name to Penarol, after the district in which the railway offices were based.

The Thingummy FC quiz

Penarol are just one of many clubs (like Manchester United and Arsenal) whose names have changed in some way since they were founded. Use this set of well-known club names to replace the word THINGUMMY in the facts that follow.

a) THINGUMMY are the sports club of the electronics company, Philips.

b) Annoyed that their club was refusing to accept foreign players as well as the home-grown variety, a group of rebels broke away to form THINGUMMY.

c) They got their name because one of the club's founders saw THINGUMMY printed on the side of a container that had just been unloaded from a ship.

d) THINGUMMY was copied! It was the name of an English rugby club of the time.

e) You can't call your team THINGUMMY unless you've got supporters in high places – or, rather, high palaces!

f) This team was formed by a group of young students so it made sense for them to choose the name THINGUMMY.

g) English spelling wasn't the strong point of the founders of this team: their first attempt at a club name was "Footh-ball Club THINGUMMY".

Answers:
a) PSV Eindhoven. The PSV stands for Philips Sport Vereniging – that is, Philips Sports Club. They're basically a works team who've managed to win the European Cup!
b) Internazionale. – where "internazionale" means "international". It happened in 1908, nine years after the Milan Cricket and Football Club was formed. In other words, Inter Milan is the son of AC Milan! They're friends now, though – the two clubs even share a ground. For a while, though, you wouldn't have known that Inter were a Milanese team. During the 1930s the Italian government forced them to change their name to "Ambrosiana"!

c) River Plate. The club (like its great rivals, Boca Junior) was founded by immigrant dockworkers who were attracted to the game by seeing English sailors having a kick-about. That's how the name was chosen. One of the new team's players saw the name "River Plate" on the side of a ship's container and thought it would be a really dishy name for a football team!

WE TOOK OUR TEAM'S NAME FROM THE SIDE OF A CONTAINER

WE'RE CALLED FLUFFY SLIPPERS

d) Glasgow Rangers. The team was started in 1873 by three young Scots after seeing a group playing a game of football on Glasgow Green. It was one of these three, a Moses McNeil, who came up with the name "Rangers" – he'd seen it used as a team name in a book about English rugby.

e) Real Madrid. The team began life as plain old Madrid FC in March, 1902. They stayed that way until 29 June 1920. That was the day their biggest fan, King Alfonso XIII, gave them permission to stick the word "Real" (Spanish for "Royal") on the front.

I THINK THEY'RE LETTING THIS ROYAL BUSINESS GO TO THEIR HEADS!

f) Juventus. Legend has it that the club began life on a bench in Re Umberto Avenue, Turin. That's where, in 1897, a group of college students decided that starting their own football club would give them something interesting to do (obviously they didn't fancy studying!) Being young and Italian, they knew that the Latin word for young was "Juventus". The club was originally called Sports Club Juventus. Two years later the name was changed to Football Club Juventus.

FOOTBALL! FOOTBALL! FOOTBALL! DOMINOES!

g) Ajax. The dodgy spellers began by calling their team "Union", only to change it to "Footh-Ball Club Ajax". When Ajax lost the ground they played their footh-ball on, it gave the organisers a chance to put matters right. At a crisis meeting in a café on 18 March 1900, the club was re-formed as a properly spelt "Football Club Ajax".

THE POSSIBLY FOULER AND DEFINITELY MADDER NAME FOR A NEW FOOTBALL TEAM AWARD...

Colo Colo of Chile. The club was formed by five players who'd had a big argument with their previous club, Magallanes FC, and were still feeling angry about things – hence their choice of "Colo Colo". It's the Chilean nickname for a wild cat!

Shirt tales

Anybody wanting to start up a new team nowadays would have to spend ages simply discussing the details of what kind of football shirts they were going to wear! They'd have to worry about what size letters to have for the players' names, where their sponsor's logo was going to go, whether the shirts were going to have short sleeves or long sleeves, was the team's name going to be stitched on to the collar or the tail, or the collar *and* the tail ... and so on. There are so many possibilities they'd do well to find time to actually play a match!

But that's now. In football's early days life was much simpler. A football shirt didn't always look that different to a normal shirt, except that you didn't wear a tie with it.

WE MAY BE USELESS BUT NOBODY CAN SAY WE'RE NOT SMARTLY TURNED OUT!

Add a club badge, and you were there. Spanish giants Barcelona, for example, have played in their famous blue and claret colours since day one. But even they couldn't decide what to have as a club crest. So they decided to hold a competition – and the badge on their shirts today is the same design which won that competition. It was the entry of a Barcelona supporter named ... anonymous. To this day nobody knows who that competition winner was.

Feeling cross?

Italian club AC Milan don't have the same problem. They know exactly who designed the badge on their famous red-and-black striped shirts. It was one of their founders, Herbert Kilpin – a patriotic Englishman. At that time, most English club badges showed England's flag, the Cross of St George, as part of their design. Kilpin didn't see anything at all foul about copying them – so he did. That is why, to this day, AC Milan's badge includes that old red cross on a white background.

That's not to say the club are stuck in the past, though. In many ways AC Milan's shirts have been ahead of their time. In 1981 the club were the first to print their player's names on the back of the shirts. They were also the first to introduce a sponsor's name.

Seeing red

Sparta Prague of the Czech Republic were another club who thought English football shirts were anything but foul – and even if they did, the design they started with was even fouler. When the club was formed in 1893, Sparta played their early games wearing black shirts with a large "S" for "Sparta" on the front.

This changed in 1906. Their club president made a trip to England and while there he was taken to see one of Arsenal's league matches. So impressed was he by the club's red shirts he decided there and then that as far as his own team's kit was concerned it was going to be "S" for "Scrap". When he got back home Sparta changed to the red shirts they still wear.

All white!

Copying colours was seen as a perfectly fair thing to do, in fact. For a club to copy another's colours was seen as a mark of respect.

That was Real Madrid's argument, anyway. Their founders settled on a strip of white shirts and white shorts because they wanted to be just like a team from London called Corinthians. Yes, an English team! The Corinthians were a world-famous amateur team who regularly provided over half England's players in the 1890s and 1900s. What's more, no side played fairer football. If a Corinthians defender ever gave away a penalty, their goalkeeper would refuse to try and save the kick.

Wrong? Right!

Italian club Juventus were another who changed their shirts because of the English influence. The difference in their case was that it happened by mistake!

After their formation in 1900, the team had started out wearing pretty pink shirts. Three years later they must have been wearing thin, because the decision was taken to order a new set from the manufacturers in England. Back came the parcel – only for the club to discover that they'd been sent the wrong set. Instead of the colour Juventus had ordered, the shirt-makers had sent a set intended for the English club, Notts County – in black-and-white stripes.

Were the shirt-makers left pink with embarrassment? No, because Juventus didn't complain. They liked the stripes so much they adopted them at once and have been ordering them ever since!

NOW THESE HAVE DEFINITELY GOT TO GO BACK!

SHORTS

So it looks like the English style of football shirt was regarded as a fair bet. It certainly was if you compare it to those worn by Scottish team Clyde FC in 1919.

The First World War had just ended and money was in short supply; Clyde didn't have the cash to splash out on a smart new set of shirts. All they could afford were the kind of shirts on special offer at their local army-surplus store. In went their order – and out ran the Clyde players for their next match in colours of foul sludge-brown khaki.

THE EVEN FOULER SHIRTS AWARD...

Ajax Cape Town (South Africa) whose shirts were foul enough to get them expelled from the South African Super League in October 2003. The rules said that every club had to wear shirts carrying the name of the league's sponsor, the Japanese car manufacturer Toyota. After failing to do this three times, Ajax were driven out of the league. They would have been champions.

Playing fair or playing foul?

Every famous top club had to rise from being an unknown bottom club. Here are some that managed to do just that – but was it by fair means or foul?

1 Moscow Dynamo achieved fame as the first Russian club to venture abroad when they travelled to Britain in 1945. Did the team go back home with a reputation for being **fair or foul**?

THIS IS HIS FIRST TIME ABROAD!

2 In 1992, French team Olympique Marseille were another side with money to spend. They won the French championship, then went on to win the European Cup. But had they used **fair means or foul**?

3 In the 1950s Columbian club Millonarios had a brief spell of fame by offering big money to players willing to join them. Many stars did just that and Millonarios' blue-shirted players danced round the opposition so well that they were nicknamed "the blue ballet". But were Millonarios regarded as **fair or foul**?

4 Nacional of Uruguay must hold the record for the quickest rise to top level. Formed in 1899, they'd become good enough just four years later to be sent out to represent their country. Did they do it by **fair means or foul**?

5 Dynamo Kiev were another team which became good enough to represent their country. In the qualifying competition for the 1976 European Championships, the then USSR players (Kiev is now in Ukraine) were almost all from Dynamo. What's more, as they were officially amateurs, the same players became the USSR's football team for the Olympic Games as well! But when they were formed in 1927, were Dynamo thought of as a **fair team or foul?**

Answers:

1 Fair Even though Dynamo gave their opponents a hard time – they drew with Chelsea (3-3) and Rangers (2-2), and beat Arsenal (4–3) and Cardiff (10–1!) – they impressed all who saw them with their fair play and teamwork. What's more, before each game every Dynamo player presented his opposite number with a lovely bunch of flowers!

EXPECT A HARD GAME!

R.I.P.

2 Foul It was proved that Marseille had used some of their money to bribe opposition teams not to try against them. Once the truth came out Marseille were fined, relegated – and eventually went bust.

3 Foul Millonarios were members of a Columbian "pirate" league – that is, a league which wasn't linked to an official Football Association. This meant that no team outside Columbia was allowed to play them.

4 Fair And their performance on that occasion was pretty good too. They won their match, beating deadly rivals Argentina 3–2!

5 Foul (That's what crooks thought, anyway.) Russian football teams were made up of workers who had the same sort of job during the day and Dynamo Kiev's players were all policemen! They weren't particularly good at football, either. Dynamo spent their first few seasons being overrun by the railway workers of Lokomotiv Kiev. In other words, the team that became the USSR's finest were once not even the best in Kiev!

The matches of death

Dynamo Kiev are at the centre of a story about a newly formed team which is probably part-true and part-legend – but definitely completely amazing. The story concerns the Kiev side and opponents who proved to be even fouler than anybody could imagine...

HERE ARE THE FACTS NOBODY DOUBTS:

IN AUGUST 1942, AS THE SECOND WORLD WAR SPREAD DRAMATICALLY, KIEV WAS CAPTURED BY THE GERMAN FORCES...

MANY OF THE KIEV PLAYERS (BOTH DYNAMO AND LOKOMOTIV) WERE TRAPPED...

THEY SPENT THEIR DAYS WORKING IN A KIEV BAKERY...

DURING THIS TIME THEY BEGAN PLAYING TOGETHER FOR A NEW FOOTBALL TEAM. IT WAS CALLED START F.C.

NOW WE START (HO-HO!) GETTING INTO THE DOUBTFUL BITS...

41

SOME SAY THE KIEV PLAYERS FORMED START FC THEMSELVES; OTHERS, THAT THEY WERE MADE TO DO IT BY THE GERMAN FORCES.

SOME SAY THAT START FC ARRANGED MATCHES FOR THEMSELVES; OTHERS THAT THE GERMAN FORCES MADE THEM PLAY VARIOUS TOP TEAMS THEY BROUGHT IN FROM GERMANY AND OTHER COUNTRIES THEY'D CAPTURED.

BACK TO PARTS OF THE STORY THAT EVERYBODY IS AGREED ON:

EVEN THOUGH THE KIEV PLAYERS WERE UNFIT AND HUNGRY, THE PART-TIME BAKERS ALWAYS ROSE TO THE OCCASION. THEY WON EVERY GAME THEY PLAYED.

SEEING THIS, THE SPIRITS OF THE KIEV PEOPLE ROSE AS WELL. THE TEAM WAS GIVING THEM REASON TO SMILE AGAIN.

IT'S BACK TO THE DOUBTFUL BITS, NOW. AND GET YOUR HANDKERCHIEFS READY...

IT'S SAID THAT START FC'S SUCCESSES MADE THEIR CAPTORS ANGRY – SO ANGRY THAT THEY DECIDED TO BRING IN THE BEST TEAM THEY POSSIBLY COULD. PACKED WITH GERMANY'S BEST PLAYERS, THEY WOULD CRUSH KIEV AND SHOW THEM WHO WAS BOSS.

IT'S SAID THAT THE START TEAM WERE TOLD THAT IF THEY WON THIS MATCH THEY WOULD BECOME NON-STARTERS IN THE FUTURE; THEY'D NEVER PLAY AGAIN... BECAUSE THEY'D BE DEAD.

IT'S SAID THAT THE GAME WAS PLAYED... AND THAT TO THE JOY OF THE KIEV PEOPLE, START FC FINISHED AS THEY'D STARTED AND WON YET AGAIN.

IT'S SAID THAT THE CAPTORS WERE TRUE TO THEIR WORD. ONE BY ONE THE KIEV STARS WERE TRANSFERRED FROM THE BAKERY TO CONCENTRATION CAMPS... AND NEVER CAME OUT.

EVEN FOULER FOOTBALLERS

It doesn't matter where you go, football – like all other professions – has its fair share of foul players and even fouler teams. Check out these tales to discover the sort of things they get up to. (But do *not* try them when you're playing for the school side!)

Daylight robbery

It's not unknown for teams to say their opponents have stolen the game with a last-minute goal. But it's quite unusual to have a game end with a player actually arrested for being a thief!

It happened in 1991, as the top Uruguayan teams Penarol and Nacional were doing battle. As usual Dely Valdez, Nacional's striker, was wearing the collection of valuable gold necklaces he was famous for. Against him was Penarol defender Goncalves. At one point during the match, as the two players were in a tussle near the corner flag, Goncalves whipped off one of Valdez' necklaces and hid it in his football sock. Unfortunately for the Penarol plunderer, although dozy Dely didn't spot that he was a necklace short, the TV cameras covering the match certainly did. The moment the teams left the pitch, Goncalves was arrested!

ANYONE SEEN THE LORD MAYOR'S CHAIN?

Was it gaol for Goncalves? No – he gave the necklace back and charges were dropped.

Brazilian goalkeeper Fabio Costa, on the other hand, made no attempt to hide what he'd stolen during a league match between his club Vitoria and Atletico Mineiro. In protest at having a penalty awarded against him, he took ... the match ball! When the Atletico players tried to get it back to get on with the game Fabio the Grabio beat them off with karate kicks. A big brawl followed until, after a full ten minutes, the ball was prised from Costa's clutches and the game restarted.

You're so rude!

Footballers who show off their bits (naughty or otherwise) are frowned upon nowadays. Referees can

shout "foul" and give a player a yellow card for whipping his shirt off in celebration – or for lifting it up to reveal a message underneath.

Even in the days when it wasn't a crime, not everybody thought that shirt-throwing was a clever thing to do. In 1997, after Celtic's Portuguese player Jorge Cadete threw his dirty shirt into the crowd at the end of a match, his manager Tommy Burns said:

That sort of behaviour doesn't wash with me!

A far fouler example from Brazil in 1997 showed that the opposite can occur. Paulo Mata, coach of Brazilian league side Lapertuna, showed his players how *not* to behave. Upset that three of his players had been sent off in the closing minutes of a 3–2 defeat by Vasco da Gama, Mata raced on to the field and waggled his bare bum at the referee!

Spanish club Alfacar didn't have just one player removing an item of kit – the whole team did it. What's more, they didn't stop with their shirts. They kept going until they'd removed everything else as well!

It wasn't foul play this time, though. On the contrary, it was all in a good cause. It happened in 1998, with the club desperately in need of money. So to raise funds the players came up with the idea of doing – a striptease act! They booked their town's biggest disco and started practising.

When it came to the big night, though, only 13 of the 21-strong squad of players joined the line-up. The other eight were left out because their horrified wives and girlfriends wouldn't let them take part!

Liverpool and England star Kevin Keegan also did a striptease act that wasn't foul. It wasn't even intentional. He was on the substitutes bench for England's vital World Cup qualifying match against Poland in October 1973. With England needing to win, but only drawing 1–1, Keegan was desperate to get on the pitch. So when, with just a few minutes to go, manager Sir Alf Ramsey said, "Kevin, get ready!" he didn't waste any time. He leapt to his feet while Liverpool team mate Ray Clemence pulled off his tracksuit trousers ... and, in his haste, Keegan's shorts ... and undies!

The worst was yet to come. There were two Kevins on the bench that night and Ramsey had been calling for the other one, Kevin Hector of Derby County. While Keegan hastily covered himself up again Hector went on. He just failed to score, the match ended 1–1, England went out of the World Cup and Ramsey was sacked. A bad night all round.

Insufficient effort

Nothing makes a fan more mad than the suspicion that the footballers he's paying to watch aren't playing fair and trying their hardest. In England, a Sheffield Wednesday fan named Bob Montgomerie was so disgusted with his team's pathetic performance in losing an FA Cup 6th round replay 5–1 to Southampton in 1984 that he took them to court! Perhaps remembering that when Queen Victoria died in 1901 all football grounds had been closed because they were thought of as "places of entertainment", Montgomerie said  he'd paid for his ticket expecting to be entertained – and the Sheffield Wednesday players hadn't tried to do that at all! This, he argued, meant the club had obtained his money under false pretences. Sadly the judge didn't agree.

In 1997 a VIP fan in an even fouler mood was Kamal al-Ganzuri, Egypt's prime minister. After his country's international team surprisingly lost a World Cup qualifying match to tiny Ghana, crafty Kamal decided that it would do the posing players good if they didn't see their pictures on the back pages of the daily newspapers for a while. So he personally asked editors not to publish reports of Egypt's matches for the next 50 days.

Did al-G's antics pay off? No. The editors refused to do what he'd asked – and, to make matters worse, splashed the story all over their *front* pages as well!

Trying hard isn't a lot of good if a footballer is using drugs to make it happen. It's been claimed that in 1978, foul Eastern European players took drugs under the orders of their even fouler military governments.

Players have their pee tested to detect this sort of dirty trick, of course, so to get away with it other people's pee was given to the testers instead. What made the testers think something dodgy was going on? The test on the pee, which was supposed to have come from one powerful player, showed that he was expecting a baby!

IS KLAUS PUTTING ON WEIGHT?

Sometimes footballers just can't win. If they don't try hard they get shouted at – but, in one player's case, trying too hard got him sacked!

In 2002, South Korean striker Ahn Jung-hwan played for Italian club, Perugia. At least he did until Japan surprisingly knocked Italy out of the 2002 World Cup finals, and Perugia's chairman Luciano Gaucci decided that Ahn should be gahn. Why? Because it had been action-man Ahn who'd won the match for Japan with an extra-time golden goal.

Sinister spells

Sometimes teams don't worry so much about avoiding foul play as avoiding foul luck. Either they'll try to make sure they don't suffer any – or somebody will claim to have tried on their behalf.

I CAN BEND IT LIKE URI !

England's star foul-luck-foiler is a man named Uri Geller, whose special claim to fame is his uncanny ability to bend spoons.

Useful Uri claimed to have helped hosts England reach the semi-finals of the European Championships in 1996. How? By sprinkling magic crystals at various places in Wembley Stadium. So why hadn't England gone all the way and won the title? Because, said Geller, he wasn't allowed in to sprinkle on the pitch before their match against Germany – and that's why England had lost on a penalty shoot-out.

Two years later, before England headed off to France for the 1998 World Cup finals, Uri Geller was back "helping" again. This time he said he'd energized the World Cup trophy itself, filling it full of good luck for the England team. Unfortunately he'd have done better to energize the England team. They were beaten by Argentina in another penalty shoot-out!

England may not have been helped by Uri Geller's attempt to "bend" the rules, but in Kenya some fans thought their opponents were trying an even fouler trick – with a bottle of water!

In 1995, regional league side Chememil were accused of practising juju (witchcraft) on their opponents, Agro-Chemical. How? By placing a bottle of water in the back of their goal. (Yes, water. Not even a bottle of evil spirits!) They thought it had been

charmed by an unfriendly witch doctor – a suspicion that was reinforced when Chemelil flatly refused to remove the bottle. That really convinced the Agro fans that something was going on and they stormed the pitch to cause some agro. The match was held up for half an hour as battle raged!

Similar suspicions of foul play also caused problems at an African Champions League match in 1998. When Mozambique team Ferroviaro missed a penalty against Zimbabwean side Dynamos, the home team were pretty sure they knew why. No, it wasn't because Ferroviaro had a pathetic penalty-taker, but that a spare set of goalkeeping gloves had been left beside one post of Dynamos' goal.

First a Ferroviaro player was booked for snatching the gloves to check them for magic charms. Then a voice began accusing the Dynamos' goalkeeper of being a witch doctor – over the ground's tannoy system! Not surprisingly there was a small riot between home fans and the police as the pitch was invaded and the offending gloves stolen.

Finally, there's the story of Racing Club of Argentina, who didn't simply think that one particular team were trying nasty tricks on them. Back in 1998 they were convinced that the whole underworld had it in for them and that their 32-year run of failure to win the Argentine Championship was due to evil spirits haunting their ground.

So they held a special torchlight ceremony. All their fans were told to turn up wearing their holiest (not hole-iest!) white. They then held a religious service. After that the Racing team came out to play a friendly match and prove that all was now well. It wasn't. Racing lost the match 2–0!

The porkie-pies quiz

In the summer of 2003, England star David Beckham moved from Manchester United to Real Madrid for £25 million. It was a move that both sides had been talking about for months. But had they been telling the truth? Here are just ten quotes from that period. Replace PORKIE-PIE* in each quote with the correct word from this list:

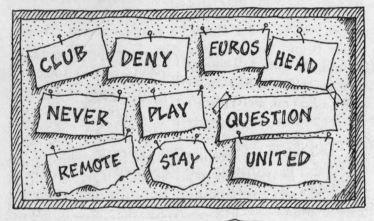

CLUB DENY EUROS HEAD
NEVER PLAY QUESTION
REMOTE STAY UNITED

ⓐ THE POSSIBILITY HE WILL ONE DAY PLAY FOR REAL MADRID IS VERY PORKIE-PIE – REAL MADRID'S MANAGING DIRECTOR, JOHN VALDANO. MARCH 27.

ⓑ IT IS TOTALLY OUT OF THE PORKIE-PIE, THERE IS NO WAY WE WOULD SELL HIM, OR ANY OF OUR BEST PLAYERS – MANCHESTER UNITED MANAGER, SIR ALEX FURGUSON, APRIL 4.

*In Cockney rhyming slang a "porkie-pie" is a lie.

ⓒ BECKS TO PORKIE-PIE – DAILY MAIL NEWSPAPER HEADLINE, APRIL 7.

ⓓ IT HAS NOT ENTERED THE PORKIE-PIE OF ANYONE AT REAL MADRID THAT BECKHAM COULD PLAY FOR REAL MADRID NEXT SEASON – REAL MADRID PRESIDENT FLORENTINO PEREZ, APRIL 6.

ⓔ WE CAN CATEGORICALLY PORKIE-PIE THAT ANY DEAL IS IN PLACE TO SELL DAVID BECKHAM TO REAL MADRID – MANCHESTER UNITED STATEMENT, APRIL 12.

ⓕ PORKIE-PIE, PORKIE-PIE, PORKIE-PIE. PORKIE-PIE NOTHING, PORKIE-PIE, PORKIE-PIE, PORKIE-PIE, PORKIE-PIE. NOT NOW. NOT EVER. REAL MADRID PRESIDENT FLORENTINO PEREZ, APRIL 29. (SAME WORD EVERY TIME!)

ⓖ I WANT TO STAY AT PORKIE-PIE – DAVID BECKHAM, MAY 6.

ⓗ I'D RATHER JACK IT IN THAN LEAVE UNITED. THEY'RE THE ONLY TEAM I'VE EVER WANTED TO PORKIE-PIE FOR – DAVID BECKHAM, THE NEWS OF THE WORLD NEWSPAPER, JUNE 15.

(i) MANCHESTER UNITED TODAY REACHED AGREEMENT FOR THE TRANSFER OF DAVID BECKHAM TO REAL MADRID FOR A FEE OF 35 MILLION PORKIE-PIE. – STATEMENT RELEASED BY MANCHESTER UNITED, JUNE 17.

(j) I KNOW THAT I WOULD ALWAYS REGRET IT LATER IN LIFE IF I HAD TURNED DOWN THE CHANCE TO PLAY AT ANOTHER GREAT PORKIE-PIE LIKE REAL MADRID. DAVID BECKHAM, JUNE 17.

Answers:
a) remote; **b)** question; **c)** stay; **d)** head; **e)** deny; **f)** never; **g)** United; **h)** play; **i)** euros; **j)** club.

So who was telling foul fibs? The player? The two clubs? Or were the newspapers which printed it all telling even fouler fibs? You'll have to decide for yourselves – but in future bear in mind this Foul Football award winner...

THE VERY TRUE AWARD...

Ivan Esar, who wasn't a footballer or a reporter, but an American writer. In 1943 he published what he called his *Comic Dictionary*. In it he provided the definition: *Truth – the only thing that you cannot add to without subtracting from.*

CONTINENTAL COMPETITIONS

If you need proof that football is the most widespread game in the world you need look no further than all the international competitions that exist nowadays. Do the English claim the credit for inventing international games too? Of course! Well ... together with Scotland, Wales and Northern Ireland they do.

The four countries were the first to play each other in a competition. Called the Home International Championship, it began way back in the 1883–84 season and lasted for 101 years. By then bigger competitions had become more important. The biggest, of course, is the World Cup which takes place every four years. Other major competitions are the European Championship, the African Nations Cup and the South American Championship. But these are all for international teams.

For club sides there are even more international competitions. What are they? Where are they? Did they begin in England, too? Find out with this tournament timeline:

1927 The Mitropa Cup begins. It's the first international club competition in the world – and England aren't involved! It's played for by the champion clubs of Austria, Czechoslovakia, Hungary, Italy, Romania, Switzerland and Yugoslavia.

1949 The Latin Cup begins. It isn't to discover which club has the most footballers who can speak Latin (there'd have been too many 0–0 draws!), but a competition between the league champions of France, Spain, Italy and Portugal. It lasts until 1957.

1955 The European FA, UEFA (which stands for *Union des Associations Européennes de Football*) are dithering over whether or not a competition could be started to include all the champion clubs in Europe. After quite a bit of prompting (see next section) they do just that – and call the competition the European Champion Clubs' Cup.

1959 The International Football Association, FIFA (it actually stands for *Fédération Internationale de Football Association),* invent the ultimate club competition, the World Club Cup. The idea is that it will be an annual match between the winners of the European Champion Clubs' Cup and the South American champions. The only problem is that South

America don't have a champions' cup. So they invent one, quick!

1960 The Liberty Cup, known in Spanish as the *Copa Libertadores da América* begins as a competition to discover the South American club champions. It's organized by the *Confederación Sudamericana de Fútbol* (known by the abbreviation CONMEBOL – work that one out if you can!).

1960 Another European club competition begins, the International Football Cup. Now known as the Intertoto Cup, it's a summer competition. Why? Because the clubs want it that way? No – because it's said that football fans want some proper matches to bet on during the summer months!

1964 The African FC Champions Cup begins. Organized by the *Confederation Africaine de Football* (CAF) it starts out as a knockout tournament between champion clubs. Nowadays it's run as a league competition.

1987 The Oceania Clubs Championship begins, run by the Oceania Football Confederation

(OFC) for club teams in the southern hemisphere. Nowadays the competition is played every two years as a tournament lasting about two weeks.

1988–1999 Clubs tournaments multiply like mad. They include tournaments like the African Cup Winners Cup for knockout cup (rather than league) champions and the UEFA Cup – a competition for best-performing league sides who haven't qualified for any other competition and want to go in for one!

2000 FIFA launches what it hopes will be the ultimate club competition for the winners of each and every federation's championships. It's called the World Club Championships and is held for the first time in Brazil. It's won by Corinthians of Brazil. Europe's champions are a team from England, called Manchester United. They're knocked out at the group stages, but simply by taking part they're once again leading the way…

We all follow Man Utd!

Since 1994, Europe's top club competition has been known as the European Champions League or "Champions League" for short. Between 1955, when it began, and 1993 it was known as the European Cup. All of which goes to show that it's perfectly possible for even the most fanatical fans to get something totally wrong for 50 years – the proper name for Europe's top competition has always been, and still is, the European Champion Clubs' Cup!

So how did anybody know who were the top European team before this competition (whatever it was called) began? The answer is, they didn't. Although the Mitropa Cup had been running for nearly 30 years, it didn't cover all the teams in Europe. As a result, any country could claim their champions were the best. And, in 1955, the English newspapers were doing just that for the Football League champions, Wolverhampton Wanderers. Were they believed? Not by one French newspaper, they weren't...

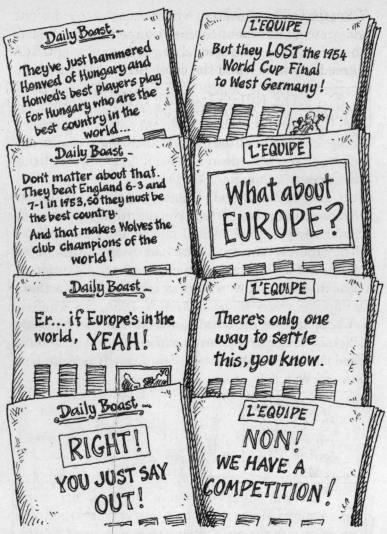

Daily Boast – They've just hammered Honved of Hungary and Honved's best players play for Hungary who are the best country in the world...

L'EQUIPE – But they LOST the 1954 World Cup Final to West Germany!

Daily Boast – Don't matter about that. They beat England 6-3 and 7-1 in 1953, so they must be the best country. And that makes Wolves the club champions of the world!

L'EQUIPE – What about EUROPE?

Daily Boast – Er... if Europe's in the world, YEAH!

L'EQUIPE – There's only one way to settle this, you know.

Daily Boast – RIGHT! YOU JUST SAY OUT!

L'EQUIPE – NON! WE HAVE A COMPETITION!

And that's how the European Cup began. Annoyed about British newspapers claiming that the English champions, Wolverhampton Wanderers, were the best club side in the world, the French newspaper

L'Equipe set up a meeting with Europe's top sides and suggested a knockout competition to decide which of them really was the best. Everybody said yes, UEFA agreed to run it – and the competition kicked off!

THE NOT-YET-GOOD-ENOUGH BEST CLUB IN THE WORLD AWARD...

Wolverhampton Wanderers. Ironically Wolves didn't qualify for the first European Champion Clubs' Cup competition – because by the time it began they were no longer league champions! When Wolves qualified next, in 1959, they were knocked out in the first round. They did better a year later, reaching the quarter-finals before losing 9–2 on aggregate to Barcelona. But they haven't won it yet or qualified for it again.

Chelsea were the team who'd beaten Wolves to the 1954–55 English league title. How many games did Chelsea lose in that first season of European Cup games? Was it...

Answer: a) But the only reason they didn't lose any was because they didn't play any! Even though they'd qualified, Chelsea decided not to take part. They'd been talked out of it by the organizers of the Football League who'd said the competition would mean them having to play too many games.

So it was left for Manchester United to show English clubs the way. A year later, after winning the 1955–56 league title, they entered the 1956–57 competition. This was in spite of them being advised, just like Chelsea, not to take part. United manager Matt Busby ignored the advice, saying:

The Continental challenge should be met, not avoided.

In their first game his team didn't just meet the challenge, they trampled all over it. They won their first home tie 10–0! The unlucky opponents were Anderlecht of Belgium. United could have won by more but the players spent the last part of the game trying, unsuccessfully, to make a goal for winger David Pegg who was the only outfield player not to score!

What made the victory even more spectacular was that the "home" match hadn't been played at United's own ground, Old Trafford, but at Maine Road, the ground of their local rivals Manchester City. Competition rules said that matches had to be played under decent floodlights and in 1955 Old Trafford didn't have any! They were still being constructed.

Those weren't the days of pampered stars, either. An away tie in Spain against Atletico Bilbao was played in thick snow. Worse, after losing 5–3, the United players then had to help shovel snow from the airport runway so that their aeroplane could take off and get them home! They'd all thawed out by the second leg, though, winning 3–0 to take the tie 6–5 on aggregate.

United had reached the semi-final. Now they met another Spanish team – and were beaten 3–1 in the first leg match. Back they came for the return leg under the (now built) Old Trafford floodlights. In a ding-dong game, Manchester United were held to a 2–2 draw, which meant they were out of the competition 5–3 on aggregate.

They'd been beaten by the most famous team that European club competition has ever seen: Real Madrid.

White hot – Real Madrid

Real Madrid had come a long way since their club offices had been the back room of a shop and they'd changed into their famous white shirts in a tavern. By 1955 they were the top team in Spain. For the next five years nobody could argue that they were also the top team in Europe. Why not? Because marvellous Madrid won the competition every single year! Here's their record:

1955-56: Beat Reims (France) 4-3

1956-57: Beat Horentina (Italy) 2-0

1957-58: Beat AC Milan (Italy) 3-2

1958-59: Beat Reims (France) 2-0

Then, in 1959–60, Real won their way through to their fifth final in a row.

The game took place at Hampden Park in Scotland, against Eintracht Frankfurt of West Germany (who'd routed Rangers, the Scots' own champions, 12–4 on aggregate in their semi-final).

Here's how to recreate the game in the playground:

● Pick a couple of teachers to play for you. One has to be a bit bald and 33 years old. Call him Alfredo di Stefano. He's got a really powerful left-footed shot, which he gives his dad the credit for by saying:

> *I was right-footed, so my father didn't let me play unless I would shoot the ball with my left foot.*

● The other teacher also has to be 33 years old. He's not bald, but he is short and pudgy. Call him Ferenc Puskas.

- Once the game starts, don't do anything for 19 minutes. Then let the other team score.

- Now start to play. With you all playing your part, awesome Alfredo equalizes and then hits a second.

- Fabulous Ferenc has to join in now. He bangs in a goal before half time, then, after a nice cup of tea, another two in the second half to complete his hat trick!

You're not finished yet. The game needs another four goals ... and keep an eye on your watch because they have to be scored in four minutes! Ferenc again, then the other team, then Alfredo to complete his own hat trick, then a last goal for the other team.

● After 90 minutes, grab your calculators and work out what the score is! You should end up with:

REAL MADRID
7
EINTRACHT FRANKFURT
3

That amazing win was to see the end of their glorious run. The following year they were knocked out by deadly Spanish rivals Barcelona. But their five victories in a row has never been equalled. Here are five not-at-all-foul facts about those five fantastic seasons:

1 In their 37 European Cup games, Real scored 112 goals.

2 Reims' best player in the 1956 final was a Frenchman named Raymond Kopa – so Madrid bought him! He picked up winners' medals from then on.

3 It was a European Cup semifinal home leg on 11 April 1957 that saw Real Madrid's attendance record broken. The visitors (and losers) were Manchester United.

4 The 1960 final was the only one in which Hungarian hero Ferenc Puskas won a winner's medal for Real. He joined the club in 1958, but missed the 1959 final. His only other final appearance was in 1962, when Real were beaten 5–3 by the Portuguese team Benfica. It was some appearance, though: poacher Puskas scored all three Real goals.

AIM ME AT THEIR GOAL

5 Argentinain, Alfredo di Stefano – nicknamed "the white arrow" – scored in every one of Real Madrid's five winning finals.

The World Club Championship

In 1959, somebody had a bright idea. Why not have a trophy played for by the winners of the European Cup and the winners of the South American equivalent? There was only one problem with this bright idea: South America didn't have an equivalent competition.

This was easily solved. They invented one, called it the *Copa Libertadores,* and a year later Penarol of Uruguay were crowned South American champions. Everything was now ready for the big match to be played. And, as it was obviously going to be the biggest game between the biggest clubs of the two biggest football-playing continents, there seemed no point in calling it anything less than the World Club Cup.

Fittingly, Real Madrid became the first "world champions" in 1960 in Montevideo, winning the two-legged tie by whacking Penarol 5–1 in Madrid after drawing 0–0 in Montevideo. And, for the next few years, the annual match was a success. Between 1967 and 1971, though, something went horribly wrong. The matches became so violent that the competition should have been called The World Club-Each-Other-As-Much-As-Possible Cup.

This chapter started with a timeline. Well here's another one all about the World Club Championship. However, as in many of the games themselves, bits and pieces have flown about everywhere. As a result, the underlined sections have ended up in the wrong sentences and you have to sort out the trouble!

1967 Celtic of Scotland meet Racing Club of Argentina.

a) As the teams come out for the start of the second-leg game, Celtic's goalkeeper Ronnie Simpson is <u>sent off in each leg</u>.

b) After both teams won a match each, there had to be a play-off game. In this game there were so many fights that at one point the players had to be <u>sent off</u>!

c) In this match <u>their opponents</u> were sent off!

d) Things got so confusing that one player finished the game even though he'd been <u>hit by a missile</u>.

1968 Manchester United play Estudiantes de la Plata of Argentina.

e) Estudiantes have already gained a reputation for dirty tricks in the *Copa Libertadores* – their players have even been known to stick pins in <u>five players</u>.

f) In two bad-tempered matches, United have a player <u>suspended on the orders of the President</u>.

1969 It's AC Milan's turn to face Estudiantes.

g) They manage to win 4–2 on aggregate, even though in Argentina their striker Nestor Combin <u>refused to take part</u>.

h) After the game, three Estudiantes players are <u>kept apart by armed police</u>.

1970 Estudiantes again, this time against Feyenoord of Holland. The Dutch side triumph in another dirty match.

i) Their winning goal is scored by Joop van Deale in spite of the fact that he <u>has his nose broken</u>.

j) 1971–1980 The competition goes into decline because nearly every European champion <u>has broken glasses</u>.

a) As the teams come out, Celtic's goalkeeper Ronnie Simpson is hit by a missile. He had to be carried off and didn't play in the match.

b) At one point the players had to be kept apart by armed police. The ground looked more like a riot zone than a football pitch!

c) In this match <u>five</u> players were sent off! Two were from Racing Club and three from Celtic.

d) One player finished the game even though he'd been sent off! It was Celtic's Bertie Auld. After being sent off close to the end, he refused to leave the pitch. Rather than argue with him, the Paraguayan referee decided to finish the match.

e) Estudiantes players have even been known to stick pins in their opponents. Talk about giving the other side the needle!

f) United have a player sent off in each leg – Nobby Stiles in the away match and George Best at home. United lost 2–1 on aggregate.

g) AC Milan's striker Nestor Combin has his nose broken.

h) Three Estudiantes players are <u>suspended</u> on the orders of the President. Not only that, they're thrown into prison for a while.

i) Feyenoord's winning goal is scored by Joop van Daele in spite of the fact that he has <u>broken</u> glasses. Yes, he wore spectacles during matches and Estudiantes obviously thought it would be a good idea to bust them – only to learn that Joop found it no big Deale!

j) Virtually all the European champions refused to take part.

Yes, throughout the 1970s European Cup winners such as Ajax, Bayern Munich, Liverpool and Nottingham Forest all stayed at home rather than risk the foulest of games. The cup was about to die. Then, dashing to the rescue, came a saviour from – where?

Answer: c) Deciding that it would be a good way of bringing top-class football to Japan (and getting their company name widely advertised, of course) Japanese car manufacturer Toyota saved the World Club Cup in 1980 by becoming its sponsor. They lay down just one important condition: the match must always be played in Japan! Without foul and fanatical home fans urging their teams to be even fouler than their opponents, the trophy (now called the Toyota European/South American Cup) has been happily played for ever since with hardly a hint of trouble.

THE DON'T TRY TO FOUL ME IN A BIG GAME AWARD...

Jose Aguas (Benfica). Sharp-shooting Jose played for Portuguese champions Benfica when they became the first club to beat Real Madrid and win the European Cup. Legend has it that before leaving his country, Angola, to become a professional footballer, he had been a lion-hunter!

REFS RULE, OK!

Who'd be the poor referee having to cope with the sort of foul behaviour the World Club Cup produced? In fact, who'd be a referee? The man in the middle is given no end of trouble the world over.

That wasn't always the way. When organized football began using the English rules, referees weren't in the middle of the pitch at all. They would be at the side of the pitch, looking on, rather like a cricket umpire. They worked in a similar way to cricket umpires, too. If a player thought a foul had been committed or a goal scored, he would appeal. The referee would then either stop the game or, if he disagreed with the appeal, tell the teams to play on.

The people who understood the English rules best, of course, were the English. It's no surprise, then, that the best-known referee from those early days was an Englishman...

The royal ref

Referees are usually called foul
names, so the first unusual fact
about John Lewis is that he was
actually given a nice name
because he was so fair. They
called him "The Prince of
Referees". He started off as a

player with Blackburn Rovers, a club he also helped
to found, only becoming a referee after a skating
accident forced him to give up playing. Nobody ever
questioned John's judgement by accusing him of
being a cheat. Lewis was as upright as they came. He
didn't smoke, drink or gamble – and he donated all
his refereeing fees to charity! Lewis refereed three FA
Cup Finals (1895, 1896, 1897). Although he "retired"
in 1905, he was often invited to get his whistle out
again. He was still blowing it fifteen years later, in
1920, when he refereed the Olympic Games football
final between Belgium and Spain – at the age of 65!

No-nonsense Howcroft

Jack "Jimmy" Howcroft looked
more like a bank manager than
an international-class referee.
When he walked out to referee
the 1920 FA Cup Final between
Aston Villa and Huddersfield
Town he was wearing shorts to

his knees, a white shirt, a bow tie and a smart black
jacket with a white handkerchief in the top pocket!

He stood for no nonsense, though, and the players
knew it. Villa's captain that day was a hard

man named Frank Barson. Howcroft gave him an early warning, saying: "The first wrong move you make, Barson, off you go." How early? In the changing rooms before the game began! It worked, too. Barson was as good as gold and Howcroft had an easy game.

Dan, Dan the karate man

One of the best-known English referees in the modern game is Uriah Rennie. Players don't mess with him either, because as a kickboxing instructor and karate black belt 1st dan, rock-hard Rennie is tougher and fitter than they are! He's also a magistrate in his home town of Sheffield, so he knows a bit about dishing out a punishment to fit the crime. He doesn't care what the fans shout, either. He once said, "To go to Old Trafford or Highbury and referee games is not pressure. That's an honour."

The ball juggler

So did refereeing skills travel overseas in the same way as playing skills? Of course. The referee for the first-ever World Cup final in 1930 was a Belgian, John Langenus. He had to make a big decision before a ball was even kicked – whose ball were they going to play with? Uruguay

75

and Argentina had reached the final and both wanted to play the match with a ball made in their own country. So how did Juggler John resolve the problem? By playing one half of the match with each ball!

That was an easy decision compared to one Langenus had been asked to make while attempting to qualify as a referee. The examination paper asked him to imagine what he would do if he was in charge of a game during which the ball was kicked high in the air and landed in the cockpit of a passing aeroplane. Langenus didn't know – and failed the exam! He told this story years later in his autobiography. At that time the most famous referee in the world, John Langenus couldn't resist adding that in all the games he'd refereed he'd never once had the ball stolen by a thieving pilot.

A shining example

In the modern game, most agree that Italian referee Pierluigi Collina is the best in the world. Players are taking a big risk if they swear at Pierluigi, because the chances are he'll understand them. Apart from Italian, he speaks English, Spanish and 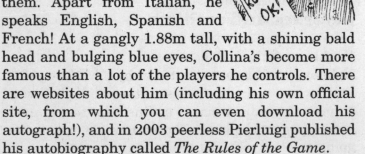 French! At a gangly 1.88m tall, with a shining bald head and bulging blue eyes, Collina's become more famous than a lot of the players he controls. There are websites about him (including his own official site, from which you can even download his autograph!), and in 2003 peerless Pierluigi published his autobiography called *The Rules of the Game*.

. Asked in an interview
t cameras and computer
a good way of resolving
es Collina shook his hairless
match should be refereed by
s."

dle

alled the referee "the man
may have to get used to

CRYING WON'T
HELP...

e
e a
petition
she took
EFA Cup
-leg match
Solna of
Fylkir of

es and ruffians

ns

es expect to get shouted at by the crowd. After
ey can't win. Any decision they make in favour
e team is a decision against the other team.
things they get from spectators are even fouler,
h...

77

- In 1996 a match b[...] Penarol and Danubio [...] crowd began throwing [...] referee ignored the sto[...] carry on after one of his lin[...] by a crash helmet!
- English referee Paul Durkin[...] during a match at Oldham i[...] at his shirt, he saw it cove[...] blood. To his great reli[...] wasn't. It was tomato [...] hot dog!
- But perhaps the most [...] a referee came from a [...] fan of Scottish club Ar[...] that his team had just ra[...] league match against East [...] on to the pitch and gave the ref[...] it appreciated? By the referee, pe[...] anybody else. Sad Sye was ba[...] ground for a year for invading the [...]

HOW DARE YOU KISS MY HUSBAND WITHOUT PERMISSION

THE LET'S-
HUMANS

Pierluigi Collina
whether he thoug
technology would be
disputes during ga
head and said, "A
men, not by machine

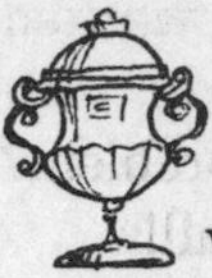

The woman in the mid
Commentators have often c
in the middle". Soon they
referring to the woman in
the middle. On 14 August
2003 Nicole Petignat made
history by becoming th
first woman to refere
UEFA men's com
match, when
charge of the U
qualifying first
between AIK
Sweden and
Iceland.

Refere

Foul fa
Refere
all, th
of o
Som
tho

etween Uruguayan sides
was abandoned after the
things at the officials. The
es and coins but refused to
esmen was knocked out

had a nasty fright
1999. Looking down
red in what looked like
ef he quickly realized it
ketchup. He'd been hit by a

unexpected thing aimed at
man named Sye Webster, a
broath. So happy was Sye
ttled in five goals in their
Stirling, that he raced
eree a big kiss. Was
rhaps, but not by
nned from the
pitch!

Fouler footballers

Ricky Rubbish can make as many mistakes as he likes, but just let him spot a referee slipping up and he'll be giving him a hard time. Some players don't stop at talking, though...

- Maybe because he'd heard about referee Pierluigi Collina's command of languages, AC Milan defender Jose Chamot didn't say a word at the end of their match against Juventus in 1998. He simply marched up, shook Collina's hand ... and earned himself a one-match ban for dissent. Why? Milan had lost 1–0 and Chamot, none too pleased, had done his best to crush the ref's fingers!

- At least Chamot could argue that he was being over-friendly. Goalkeeper James Nanoor, playing in a 1999 African Champions League match, had no defence when he spat in the face of referee Zinco Zeli. He received a one-year ban.

- It happens at all levels of the game. Somerset Sunday-league player Lee Todd was sent off for using foul and abusive language after just two seconds of a match in 2000. Why? He claimed the referee had blown the whistle too close to his ear!

- Some players don't know when to stop. Bolivian international Limberg Gutierrez was suspended for five months after head-butting the referee of his club Blooming's league match against Wilsterman in 2001. He appealed against the punishment, arguing that other players who'd done the same to a referee hadn't been banned for so long!

- He should have thanked his lucky stars he wasn't Luigi Coluccio, suspended for nine days after being sent off in an Italian local league match. Coluccio didn't serve the ban – but only because he was shot dead in a mafia-linked gun battle not long after.

> ## THE YOU'RE-STILL-BANNED-EVEN-THOUGH-YOU'RE DEAD AWARD...
> **Luigi Coluccio** who still had his ban added to his club's record even though he wasn't alive to serve it. The league organizers said it could influence which team won the league's fair play award that season!

- Maybe referees should take a tip from English referee Peter Rhodes. He had no trouble from the Los Angeles Toros and Atlanta Braves teams when he was in charge of their match in the USA league in 1978. Maybe that was because both teams knew he had a gun in his pocket! It was there because one of the odd league rules required him to fire shots two minutes before the end of each half to let everybody know how the time was going.

YOU'RE SUPPOSED TO FIRE IT IN THE AIR!

Diabolically difficult decisions

Whether or not fans and players like their decisions, it's a referee's job to make them. Not simply during the game, either. Their first job is to decide whether to start a match at all. Then, once the game has started, they have to decide when to finish it! Sounds easy? Get your whistle out, then, and have a go at making some diabolically difficult decisions!

Let's start in England (where else?)...

1 It's 1888 and you're in charge of a big FA cup fifth round tie between Aston Villa and Preston North End. After the crowd invade the pitch for the fourth time, Preston complain that they can't be expected to play an important cup match like this. **Continue or abandon?**

2 You're in charge of another FA Cup first round tie, this time between Grimsby Town and Southern League side Croydon Common in 1911. The Croydon players have been slipping over on the pitch and at half-time they spend over 20 minutes putting new studs in their boots. **Continue or abandon?**

3 It's Easter Monday, 1915, and you're Mr H Smith, refereeing Oldham Athletic v Middlesbrough in the old First Division (now the Premiership). In the second half you decide to send off Oldham's Billy Cook after he commits a couple of bad fouls. He refuses to go. You pull out your watch and give him one minute to get off. A minute later he's still there. **Continue or abandon?**

Now to discover whether you're a world-class decision-maker…

4 It's 1906 and you're about to start an international match when the Lord Mayor of London strolls on to the pitch arm-in-arm with a French film starlet and the President of the United States. The Lord Mayor insists that his guests both use one foot each to take the kick-off. **Start or don't start?**

5 It's 1949 and it's getting really dark – so dark that the players in the match you're refereeing are having trouble seeing the brown leather ball. You're about to abandon the game when suddenly a white ball is produced. **Continue or abandon?**

6 You're in charge of the Scotland v Austria match on 8 May 1963 at Hampden Park. It's supposed to be a friendly, but you've already sent off one Austrian for spitting, and another for a waist-high tackle. There are still 11 minutes to go. **Continue or abandon?**

7 It's 11 July 1966 and you're Hungarian referee Istvan Szolt. It's a big day. You're to be in charge of the World Cup Group 1 match between England and Uruguay at Wembley. However, the rules say that the players of both teams are supposed to show you their special identity cards but seven of England's well-known stars have left theirs behind. **Start or don't start?**

8 It's 1994 and you're about to referee a big international match between Portugal and Germany. You speak Portuguese and German, but no English. **Start or don't start?**

Answers:
1 Continue ... but you announce that the match won't count as a cup-tie, only a friendly. (Referees were *really* powerful in 1888!) After they'd won the game 3–1, though, Preston changed their minds. They wanted the result to count as a cup win.

SOME FRIENDLY!

Villa argued back that they'd played most of the game as a friendly! In the ensuing row, the FA came down on Preston's side. Why? Because, they said, Villa were responsible for the fans who'd caused all the trouble!

2 Continue ... but it should have been Abandon. The FA say that a half-time interval can't last longer than 20 minutes and order the game to be replayed – even though innocent Grimsby won the match 3–0. They make Croydon pay for it in the replay. This time they win 8–1!

3 Abandon. Mr Smith marched off the field and took the two teams with him. Oldham were fined £350 (worth about £16,500 today) and Cook was suspended for a year.

4 Start. It wasn't until 1907 that a rule was introduced saying that an official match had to be kicked-off by one of the players involved!

5 Abandon. You don't have any choice. The rules didn't allow games to be played with a white ball until 1950!

THE SUPER SAVER'S AWARD...

Liverpool FC who, according to goalie Tommy Lawrence (their super saver of the 1950s), wouldn't fork out for an expensive white ball but slopped white paint onto a normal one. If bits came off during a match they'd just dab some more on before the next game!

QUICK-DRYING PAINT'S EXPENSIVE AS WELL!

6 Abandon. Both sides had been at it and the referee, Jim Finney, said afterwards, "I felt that I had to abandon the match or somebody would have been seriously hurt."

7 Start. But only after Szolt made England trainer Harold Shepherdson race back to the team hotel to get the identity cards!

8 Don't start. In fact, you should really send yourself off! In 1992 the world football governing body FIFA ruled that all international referees had to be able to speak English.

YOU KNOW THE RULES. NOW OFF YOU GO!

Red card rumpuses

Spotting infringements is another part of the tough job a referee has. "Was that tackle a foul?" he has to ask. If so, was it a foul worth a yellow card? Or was it an even fouler foul worthy of a red card?

At least with coloured cards to wave the player concerned won't be in any doubt about what the referee's decided. And where did the idea of red and yellow cards come from? You've guessed it – England!

The man who gave them the green light was ex-referee Ken Aston. When the 1966 World Cup was held in England he'd retired from the middle and was in charge of the team of referees. He was forced to step forward, though, when the Argentina v England game turned out to be the foulest match of the whole tournament. German referee Rudolf Kreitlein tried to send off Argentina's non-German-speaking captain Antonia Rattin – who refused to leave the pitch until Aston, using his schoolboy Spanish, finally made him understand.

Driving home afterwards, Aston was still thinking of how referees could leave players in no doubt about what they'd decided when he was stopped by a red traffic light ... which then switched to yellow ... and promptly turned on a light in Aston's head! Red and yellow cards were on the way in.

So, red and yellow cards help a referee make his decisions clear. But, as these international stories show, that isn't always the end of the matter...

Hot meal

Referees always take a spare watch and pencil onto the pitch with them. They don't expect to need a spare red card – but when the referee in charge of the 1989 Italian league match between Pianta and Arpax showed his to Pianta's Fernando d'Ercoli, it was the last he saw of it. Furious Fernando snatched the card from his hand – and ate it!

CAN I HAVE THE YELLOW FOR AFTERS?

Diving exhibition

An equally foul, if not even fouler Italian, was Paulo Di Canio. After referee Paul Alcock sent him off while playing for Sheffield Wednesday against Arsenal in 1998, demented Di Canio shoved Alcock in the chest.

To make matters even worse he accused the referee of diving! "It was just a slight push," said potty Paulo, "and he took two or three paces back and fell over!" The English FA weren't convinced. They banned Di Canio for 11 matches and fined him £10,000.

Take that!

Unlike Alcock, Chilean first-division referee Francisco Camaano wasn't prepared to take things lying down. During an argument that took place in the last minute of a match between Deportes Temuco and Audax Italiano in July 2002, Audax's Alejandro Carrasco made the mistake of stamping on Camaano's foot. The referee didn't hesitate. Instead of wasting time fishing for his red card, cruncher Camaano promptly kneed the offending player between the legs! "It was self-defence!" he claimed, as agonized Alejandro rolled around the pitch. Camaano realized he'd done wrong, though. After the game he announced his retirement from refereeing – much to the relief of players everywhere!

I cannot tell a lie

Another official who wasn't too proud to admit he'd made a mistake was English referee Stephen Lodge, in 1993. After realising he'd sent off the wrong player during a league match between Oxford United and Sunderland, solemn Stephen knew what he had to do. The next day he wrote to the Football Association – and reported himself!

Flag-unhappy

Amateur matches can produce just as many red card rumpuses for referees. When Peppermill met the Gardeners Arms in the Blackpool Sunday Alliance League in 1996, a touchline collision between Gardeners Arms striker Tim Yeo and a linesman ended up with the referee giving a red card to ... the linesman! A Peppermill supporter doing the job as a volunteer, he'd taken offence at being flattened and hit Yeo over the head with his flag!

The nutty nettings game

But perhaps the trickiest call for a referee is that of deciding when a goal has been scored. Usually it's easy. The net bulges, the goalkeeper buries his head in his hands before getting up to blame his defenders (who are all holding their heads in their hands and/or blaming the goalkeeper) and all is clear-cut. But sometimes ... well look at the next two pages and see for yourself by having a go at this goal-grabbing game.

For each question simply decide "goal" or "no goal". Will you hit the back of the net or hammer the ball over the bar? Time to put on your shooting boots!

① WEDNESDAY (THE CLUB OFFICIALLY CHANGED THEIR NAME TO SHEFFIELD WEDNESDAY IN 1929 BUT PRIOR TO THIS WERE KNOWN AS THE WEDNESDAY) V BOLTON, 1885. WHEN WEDNESDAY GET THE BALL IN THE NET THE REFEREE CHEERS. GOAL OR NO GOAL?

② BADALONA V TARRAGONA, SPANISH CUP, 1983. REBOLLO OF BADALONA RUNS IN TO TAKE A PENALTY – AFTER WHICH SANTIAGO OF TARRAGONA GIVES HIM A HUG. GOAL OR NO GOAL?

③ BARNSLEY V MANCHESTER UNITED, FA CUP FOURTH ROUND, 1938. FRANK BOKAS OF BARNSLEY TAKES A THROW-IN. UNITED'S GOALKEEPER TOM BREEN JUST TOUCHES THE BALL BUT IT GOES OVER HIS HEAD AND INTO THE UNITED NET. GOAL OR NO GOAL?

④ TOTTENHAM HOTSPUR V HUDDERSFIELD TOWN, THE OLD FIRST DIVISION, 1951-52 SEASON. EDDIE BAILY OF TOTTENHAM TAKES A CORNER AND HITS THE REFEREE ON THE BACK MAKING HIM FALL FLAT ON HIS FACE! THE BALL REBOUNDS TO BAILY WHO CENTRES FOR STRIKER LEN DUQUEMIN TO SCORE. GOAL OR NO GOAL?

(5) CELTIC V FALKIRK, SCOTTISH DIVISION 'A', 1953. CELTIC'S CHARLIE TULLY SCORES DIRECT FROM A CORNER - BUT WHILE HE WAS TAKING THE KICK THERE WERE SOME SPECTATORS ON THE PITCH.

GOAL OR NO GOAL?

(6) TAGHMON V TOMBRUCK UNITED, IRISH WEXFORD LEAGUE. TAGHMON'S GOALIE SHANE KEHOE SWOOPS TO MAKE A SAVE. AS HE DOES SO, HIS BASEBALL CAP FALLS OFF. KEHOE STEPS BACK, PICKS IT UP, THEN BOOTS THE BALL UPFIELD. GOAL OR NO GOAL?

(7) ECUADOR V VENEZUELA, 1996 OLYMPIC GAMES QUALIFYING MATCH. AS ECUADOR'S DEFENDER MATAMBA TAKES A PENALTY HIS BOOT COMES OFF. BOOT AND BALL BOTH SAIL INTO THE VENEZUELA NET.

GOAL OR NO GOAL?

(8) EARL'S COLNE RESERVES V WIMPOLE 2000, ESSEX LEAGUE, 2002. THE REFEREE'S FOOT COMES INTO CONTACT WITH THE BALL AND IT GOES INTO THE EARL'S COLNE NET.

GOAL OR NO GOAL?

(9) BOLTON WANDERERS V EVERTON, FA CARLING PREMIERSHIP, 1997. BOLTON'S GERRY TAGGART FIRES IN A HEADER WHICH LOOKS TO HAVE CROSSED THE LINE. THE BOLTON TEAM SHOUT "GOAL"; EVERTON'S SHOUT "NO GOAL". THE LINESMAN THINKS "NO GOAL" TOO. WHAT DOES THE REFEREE DECIDE? GOAL OR NO GOAL?

Answers:

1 Goal. Wednesday were amateurs, Bolton professionals. As being paid for playing football was frowned on in 1885, referees often favoured the amateurs!

2 No goal, twice over. Tarragona hugged Rebello because he'd missed the penalty. The referee booked him for ungentlemanly conduct and ordered the kick to be taken again. Rebello did – and missed again.

GREAT PENALTY!

3 Goal. If the United 'keeper hadn't touched the ball it wouldn't have counted, but as he did it went down as an own goal.

4 No goal. A referee doesn't count as a player, so Baily can't touch the ball again until some other player has. Unfortunately, with his nose in the mud, the referee assumed that's what had happened – so he gave the goal and Tottenham won the match 1–0!

5 No goal. Correctly, the referee disallowed it. So Tully just shrugged, took the corner again – and scored again!

6 Goal. Correctly, the referee gave a goal. After the goalie's cap had fallen off, the wind had blown it over his goal line and into the net. Shtupid Shane had still been holding the ball when he went to collect it!

7 Goal – but the referee wrongly said "No goal" and ordered the kick to be retaken. He then made another mistake as Matamba's boot flew off again, this time hitting a post while the ball hit the crossbar. Instead of ordering yet another kick, the referee waved play on – and Ecuador lost the match 5–2.

8 Goal. Wimpole were losing 18–1 ... so, feeling sorry for them, referee Brian Savill deliberately scored to make it 18–2! Taking a dim view of this generosity, the FA banned him for seven weeks. Wimpole were happy, though – Savill's goal had made the referee their joint top scorer!

9 Goal. That's what the all-seeing TV cameras later proved. Unfortunately, referee Stephen Lodge had said "No goal" causing Bolton to draw 0–0 instead of winning 1–0. Did it matter? Yes. At the end of the season Bolton were relegated on inferior goal difference – to Everton!

THE AIR-TODAY-GONE-TOMORROW AWARD...

Every Referee. According to the rules of football, if the ball hits the referee it's as if it hasn't happened. The referee has to be treated as "air"!

PUFF!

92

Gone away

What with all the foul pressures and even fouler abuse they face, it's a wonder that referees turn up to do their job at all. So let's end this chapter with a couple of examples of times when they really haven't turned up.

Liverpool were playing Huddersfield Town at Anfield in the old First Division in 1948. The first half had finished and everybody had trooped off for the break. Then...

The whistle had been blown by somebody in the crowd.

On that occasion it was an accident that the referee wasn't around. Sometimes they really do go slow on purpose.

- In December 1998, Albanian referees deliberately started matches 15 minutes late in protest at the abuse they were getting.
- The Halifax Referee's Society in West Yorkshire had gone even further in 1995. They'd held a strike, causing 50 matches to be called off!

So why do referees do it? Because, foul as it can be, they love the game. And, let's face it, football would be even fouler without them!

THE DEVOTION TO YOUR HUSBAND EVEN THOUGH EVERYBODY ELSE WOULD LIKE TO WRING HIS NECK AWARD...

Mrs Stephen Lodge, referee's wife. When asked in an interview why he does the job, English referee Stephen Lodge said:

I enjoy it – and my wife's very keen. She's my number one supporter. She's probably my only supporter!

CRAFTY COACHING

Players have to play (foul or otherwise), but it's the manager/coach whose job it is to tell them how to play.

NO, YOU CAN PLAY SNAKES AND LADDERS AFTER YOU'VE BEATEN MANCHESTER UNITED.

So, where did the idea of football tactics come from? England, along with plenty of other ideas? The answer to that is ... not likely!

In England, the man in charge of the team was called a "manager". That's because he managed things, like buying and selling players and arguing about how much (or how little to pay them). The idea of a manager telling players how to play was seen as very odd − even by the managers themselves. England's first-ever international manager, Walter Winterbottom, wasn't appointed until 1946 (74 years after England's first game!). Even then, he didn't talk about tactics. In those days wall-to-wall TV coverage wasn't around, so Walter would concentrate on telling the players about their opponents − because he was the only one who'd seen them play!

Top tactics were far more advanced outside England. There, the man in charge of the team was called a "coach" – because his main job was seen as coaching the players. And the best coaches didn't simply devise tactics that suited their players; they devised tactics that nobody had ever thought of before. That way the opposing coaches didn't have the tactics to tackle their tactics, if you get the idea. No? Here are some world-famous examples.

Helenio's hell

Helenio Herrera was coach at Internazionale of Milan (known as Inter) in the 1960s. His terrible tactics were based on the theory that if you don't let a goal in then you only need to score one to win – and even if you don't manage that, you still won't lose! In other words, Inter concentrated on defence. Here's how to do it with your school team:

● Pick four defenders who like making friends.
● When the match starts, get each of these defenders to be so friendly towards one of the other team's forwards that they follow them everywhere. This is called man-to-man marking.

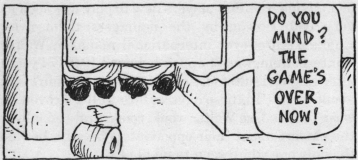

DO YOU MIND? THE GAME'S OVER NOW!

● Choose another defender who wants to be a cleaner when s/he grows up.

- Call this defender a "sweeper". His/her job is to patrol behind the four friendly defenders and be ready to run over and deal with any attacker who manages to get away from his friendly defender.
- Finally, find a goalkeeper with a large supply of warm underwear. With this tactic s/he won't have anything to do, and might get chilly with all the standing about.

Helenio's hellish system was known as *catenaccio* – the door bolt – because it was so effective at shutting out opposing forwards. Unfortunately, it was so boring that it made fans bolt for the door!

Rinus's runabouts

If you think *catenaccio* sounds chronic then read on! Rinus Michels did too. He was the coach of Dutch team Ajax between 1965 and 1971 who, more than anyone, came up with the way to cope with defensive opponents. Here's the way to do it with your team:

- Pick ten out-field players who can't decide whether they want to be forwards, midfield men or defenders.
- Throw the team's shirts on the floor and say, "Wear any one you like. The number on the back doesn't matter!"

● Before the game starts, have the team line up roughly the way you'd expect ... with number 2 nearer to your goalkeeper than number 9.

NUMBER 2, FORWARD!

I THOUGHT I WAS 9!

I'M 9.

● But all that changes once the game begins!

● If number 2 sees an attacking chance down the left wing, s/he can go for it!

● If number 9 spots danger, s/he can rush back to help out.

● In fact, just so as long as there are always the right number of bodies in defence, midfield and attack, the players can run anywhere and everywhere!

Rinus's runabout system was called "the whirl" because the Ajax players were allowed to whirl from one position to another. This made it impossible for the man-to-man marking system of *catenaccio* to operate, of course, because the opposing defenders didn't know whom they were supposed to make friends with.

"The whirl" needed talented players who were good enough to play in any position, but that's just what Ajax had. Between 1971 and 1973 they were European Champions three years in succession, with the second being the most satisfying victory of all. They ran out 2–0 winners ... against Internazionale!

Stupid Scolari's scumbags

Don't get the idea that every continental coach was crafty and calculating. Luis Felipe Scolari, manager of Brazilian side Palmeiras in the 1990s, prided himself on being foul – and liked his players to be even fouler!

When asked in 1999 about some of the tough tackles his team were making he replied:

Nobody can afford to lose now, so I ask my players to commit more fouls in midfield.

Was Luis a lone leader in the fouling field? Not according to him:

The other coaches say they don't tell their players to do this. But the fact is that I'm stupid because I tell the truth while others lie.

Partick's partners

Every coach tries to make substitutions when things aren't going well. Their aim is always to take off a tired player and put on a fresh one, or take off an out-of-form player and put on one they hope will whack in a five-minute hat trick.

So the leaders in imaginative substitutions simply have to be Bertie Auld and Pat Quinn, joint managers of Scots club Partick Thistle. On one occasion – and even though they'd already used all their substitutes – the prickly Thistle management men decided that Partick player Jim Melrose was performing so badly they'd take him off and make do with 10 men. It worked, too. Thistle bloomed and won the match 2–1!

THE COOLEST COACH AWARD...

Vittorio Pozzo (Italy). When his team played England in Turin in 1948 things got really hot. Not only was the match played in a heat wave, but England won 4–0. At one stage valiant Vittorio was reduced to trying to keep his players cool by running up and down the touchline spraying them with water from a soda siphon!

Money managers

Club managers in England might not have led the way in tactical talking but they knew their stuff off the pitch.

Herbert Chapman, manager of Huddersfield Town and Arsenal in the 1920s and 1930s, was one of the clearest thinkers in the game. He foresaw many of the football features we now take for granted, such as floodlit matches, live commentaries and even numbers on football shirts. He knew plenty about the value of publicity, too. It was Chapman who persuaded London Transport to change the name of the underground station closest to Highbury from its original name of Gillespie Road to – you've guessed it – Arsenal. Free advertising on every single map of the underground!

Chapman knew the value of a clear head when it came to transfer deals, too. In 1928 he desperately wanted to buy England international David Jack from Bolton Wanderers and was willing to smash the transfer record of £6,500 to get him; if necessary even to pay over £10,000! (Don't laugh. Even though in today's money £10,000 is worth "only" £500,000, no football club had ever paid as much for a player.)

So off Chapman went, with his assistant, to meet the Bolton officials at the Euston Hotel in London. They arrived early...

101

So Herbert Chapman got his man. David Jack scored 25 goals in the remaining 31 matches of that season and Arsenal's all-conquering team of the 1930s were on their way.

Sadly, Chapman wasn't quite so good at managing his own health. After catching a chill in January 1934, his doctor told him to stay indoors. Instead, he went off in the freezing cold to watch Arsenal's third team play, saying, "I haven't seen the boys for a week or so." He never saw them again after that. His chill turned to pneumonia and he died three days later.

Crafty coaching's testing ten quiz

Nowadays coaches (and managers) don't stay at home any more – wherever it is. Football is a world game and coaches travel the world.

At the 2002 World Cup, for instance, Tunisia's coach was a Frenchman, so was Senegal's and so was Japan's. China's coach came from Serbia and Korea had a Dutchman in charge. Even England didn't have an Englishman leading them – their coach, Sven Goran Erikkson, came from Sweden!

So, what does it take to be a top coach? Where have the most corking coaches come from? Is this one area in which fabulous foreigners have led the field or have there been some excellent Englishmen?

Come to some decisions by making some decisions about the testing ten questions in this quiz! We'll begin with three about Englishmen:

1 Bill Lambton was a typically rugged English coach. After training English boxers in Denmark he took over at Leeds United in 1957. During one of his first coaching sessions he told the players they should be able to – what?

KICK A FOOTBALL IN BARE FEET AND NOT FEEL IT.

IMPROVE THEIR HAND-EYE COORDINATION BY TRYING TO PUNCH EACH OTHER.

STAY SUPPLE BY BOUNCING ON A TRAMPOLINE.

2 A top coach has to have confidence in his own ability. Brian Clough was a double championship winner, first in charge of Derby County, then Nottingham Forest (who also won the European Cup twice). When asked whether he thought he'd been a good manager, Clough said: "I wouldn't say I was the best manager in the business. But I was in the top…" – what?

3 A conscientious coach will support his players through thick and thicker – like Aston Villa's Graham Taylor in 2002. Explaining that his England international striker Darius Vassell wasn't going to be fit for a match because of a self-inflicted injury he added kindly, "He was only trying to be helpful." What had Darius done?

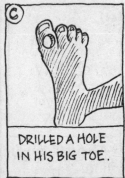

CUT A HAND WASHING HIS VILLA SHIRT

FALLEN OFF A LADDER TRYING TO MOVE A TV AERIAL TO GET A BETTER PICTURE

DRILLED A HOLE IN HIS BIG TOE.

Time to move abroad now – but only as far as Scotland for three questions about Scots coaches:

4 Coaches have to show understanding if their players get injured during a match. When Partick Thistle's John Labie was told in 1993 that his striker Colin McGlashan had sustained a head injury and didn't know who he was, Labie's immediate response was, "Tell him he's…" – what?

a) Scottish.

b) Playing for us.

c) Pele.

5 A top coach will do everything to make his players comfortable. When Liverpool arrived at their hotel the evening before their European Cup semi-final against Internazionale in 1965, their Scots manager Bill Shankly was disturbed to discover that every fifteen minutes bells would chime out loudly from a nearby monastery. What did he do to try and help his lads get a good night's sleep?

ISSUE EVERY PLAYER WITH A SET OF LIVERPOOL EARPLUGS.

ASK MONKS AT THE MONASTERY TO MUFFLE THEIR BELLS.

PLAY LOUD MUSIC TO DROWN OUT THE CHIMES.

6 A coach must convince everybody that he knows where his team is headed. Scots manager Tommy

Docherty knew exactly what to say to get the job with Rotherham United in 1967: "Chairman, I promise to take this club out of the Second Division." Did Docherty do it?
a) Yes.
b) No.

THE CONFIDENCE-BOOSTING STRAIGHT-TALKING AWARD...

Mick McCarthy, coach to the Irish Republic. After controversially sending his captain Roy Keane home from the 2002 World Cup finals, McCarthy tried – and failed – to point out that Keane wasn't a special case. "There's no difference between Roy Keane and any other player," he said, before adding, "The only difference is he's a better player."

Now three coaches who travelled to England to show the birthplace of football how to do it:

7 A top coach knows how to keep everybody happy – including himself. In 2002 Claudio Ranieri, an Italian in charge of Chelsea, said: "I am happy when our fans are happy, when our players are happy and our chairman is..." – what?

HAPPY AS A PARROT

ON THE MOON

SMILING FROM EAR TO THERE

8 A top coach doesn't let language difficulties get in the way. Frenchman Arsène Wenger faced a problem at his new club Arsenal in 1998 when his fellow countryman, striker Nicolas Anelka, told him he thought Dutch winger Marc Overmars was a load of rubbish. What did multi-lingual Wenger do?
a) Agree with Anelka.
b) Tell Overmars what Anelka had said.
c) Arrange a fight between them.

9 Not only multi-lingual, but multi-talented, Arsène Wenger showed that a top coach also has to master the art of dealing with his team's disciplinary problems. After Arsenal had finished the season with a total of nine red cards, wily Wenger said – what?
a) "We probably deserved half of them."
b) "Next season we will get less than ten."
c) "Did we? I lost count."

And, finally, a question which applies to coaches the whole world over:
10 A top coach believes in his team, come what may. After watching his Dutch league team, AZ Alkmaar, lose 5–1 at home to Roda JC in 2003, coach Co Adriaanse turned up at the post-match press conference and said of the result: "This does not mean…" – what?

Answers:

1a) Future England defender Jack Charlton promptly asked Lambton to show them how … and the coach ended up hobbling from the training pitch. A great believer in the benefits of trampolining, he got players doing **c)** as well!

2a) Clough wasn't known for his modesty.

3c) In an attempt to burst a painful blood blister, dozy Darius had drilled a hole in his toenail with a DIY electric drill! All he did was cause an infection and ended up having half his nail  removed. Oh yes … and he had to put up with the newspapers calling him the Aston Drilla!

4c) Making it the one and only time that the famous Brazilian turned out for Partick Thistle!

5b) Either they couldn't or wouldn't. Perhaps the monks were Inter fans!

6a) Unfortunately, Docherty took them in the wrong direction. Rotherham were relegated and went down to the old Third Division (now the Second Division)!

7b) What Ranieri had still to discover was that the football-speak phrase he wanted was "over the moon". Or perhaps he thought that his team still had further to go!

8b) … kind of. Both players were with him at the time, but Anelka only spoke French and Overmars didn't. So Wenger told his winger that Anelka had just said what a good player he was – and watched, beaming, as the two shook hands!

9a) Half of nine is four-and-a-half, of course. Wenger didn't manage to explain what punishment half a red card would deserve!

10c) Adriaanse then added, "That is scoreboard journalism." Strangely enough, the newspapers next day, still reported that AZ Alkmaar had lost 5–1!

What does the future hold for coaches? If developments in Italy are any clue, there's a chance it could get fairer rather than fouler. In 2003, Luciano Gaucci, President of league club AC Perugia, made it quite clear that he expected to be signing women players for his club before long – and listed the reasons why:

Women are more intelligent than men in general. They are more methodical and precise. I have seen girls playing much better than men. We have signed teenagers and they became great players. We can do the same things with girls!

So there you are – teams of the future will need womanagers!

GLOBAL GROUNDS AND DEADLY DERBIES

Nowadays the mere mention of the words "football ground" conjures up a picture of a lush green pitch surrounded by towering grandstands full of seats that cost oodles of money to sit in. But in football's early days things were very different. Pitches were just open fields, the conditions for the players were pretty foul – and any spectator who sat down risked landing on something even fouler!

THEY'RE GOING TO REGRET THROWING US OUT OF OUR FIELD!

Grounds became grander as football became more popular. Terraces were built to give fans a better view, covered areas kept the rain off, and proper seats meant the game could be watched in comfort.

As time went by, some of these football grounds became famous in their own right. They'd be remembered for the star players who'd played on their pitches and the magnificent matches they'd staged. And, sometimes, the grounds would become well known for things that had nothing at all to do with football ...

The Wembley or Highbury quiz

Two of the most famous grounds in England were Wembley Stadium, home of the England team, and Highbury Stadium, home of Premiership team Arsenal. ("Were", because they're both being knocked down! Wembley has already gone and a new Wembley is to take its place. Highbury, is expected to go the same way by 2006.) Which ground goes with each of the following facts?

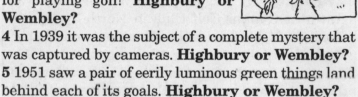

1 It was built on the remains of a college for training clergymen. **Highbury or Wembley?**

2 It was often entered by runaway dogs. **Highbury or Wembley?**

3 Its grass was specially grown – for playing golf! **Highbury or Wembley?**

4 In 1939 it was the subject of a complete mystery that was captured by cameras. **Highbury or Wembley?**

5 1951 saw a pair of eerily luminous green things land behind each of its goals. **Highbury or Wembley?**

6 An opponent once described its pitch as looking like "a comfortable bed you could lie down and sleep on". **Highbury or Wembley?**

7 There was no sleeping on duty there during World War Two! **Highbury or Wembley?**

8 It saw international boots for the first time in 1924, not to mention plenty of tricks from men who knew the ropes! **Highbury or Wembley?**

9 During the 1970s and 1980s Liverpool appeared

there so often their fans began to call it "Anfield South"! **Highbury or Wembley?**

10 It's said to be haunted by a manager's ghost. **Highbury or Wembley?**

Answers:

1 Highbury. Maybe that's why the prayers of the Arsenal fans that the score will stay at 1–0 to them, have so often been answered!

2 Wembley. From 1927 until the stadium closed in 2000, Wembley staged greyhound racing every Saturday night. Getting the stadium ready meant moving 20,000 seats to make way for the track. Such was the panic that on Cup Final day both sets of goalposts would have been removed even before the spectators had left the ground.

3 Wembley. The famously lush Wembley turf was grown at Ganton Golf Club in North Yorkshire. Once it had been laid, the Wembley ground staff would do anything to keep it looking at its best. On the morning of the Cup Final they'd all get down on their knees and weed it with dining forks!

4 Highbury. A black-and-white feature film was shot there, called *The Arsenal Stadium Mystery*. It was about a footballer who was poisoned during a match!

5 Highbury. The luminous green things were sightscreens, designed to make the white goals stand out more clearly. They were brought out if one of the dense London fogs of the 1950s was threatening to cause a match to be called off.

6 Wembley. The player was Sedun Odegbame of Nigeria, talking about the world-famous turf before his country met England in 1994.

7 Highbury. The stadium was used as an air raid patrol centre.

8 Wembley. Between 14 and 24 June 1924 it was the venue for the First International Cowboy (Rodeo) Championships.

9 Wembley. The appearances in question were those in FA Cup Finals (3 wins and 3 defeats) and season-opening Charity Shield matches (9 wins, 3 defeats), 4 League Cup Finals (4 wins and 2 defeats).

10 Highbury. It's supposed to be that of Herbert Chapman, the great Arsenal manager who died of pneumonia.

Gruesome grounds

Do you play football? Then the chances are that you've played on some foul pitches – you know, the sorts that make you think they were once a camel's graveyard. Or perhaps you've had to get changed in some even fouler dressing rooms – the kind with last year's mud on the floor and showers which do more dribbling than most wingers. Well that's the way it was for most professional players in the early days. In fact, it was like that for some of them in the not-so-early days...

I've got a sinking feeling!

In December 1961, Watford were playing Grimsby Town in an old Third Division match at their Vicarage Road ground. Playing for Watford was an ex-Tottenham Hotspur player named Tommy Harmer. Harmer was very short, just 5ft 6in (1m 67cm), but so skilful that his lack of inches had never been a problem – at least, not until that day. Then Watford won a free kick out on the right wing. Harmer ran across to take it ... only to begin disappearing down a gaping hole that had suddenly appeared in the ground!

What did Harmer say afterwards?
a) "I thought I was going to be buried alive!"
b) "It was a hole new ball game today!"
c) "I think Watford should change their name to Hole City!"

Answer: a) Harmer was a footballer not a comedian.

114

The cause of the trouble was that the ground was built on the site of an old quarry. Torrential rain the night before had soaked in to that part of the pitch and Harmer's weight had been enough to make it subside.

Was the game abandoned? No, it was just delayed while the groundsman filled the hole with several buckets of sand and then covered it with bits of grass dug from the surrounds of the pitch.

What a shower!
Top Argentinian club River Plate sailed to various home grounds before ending up at their present stadium, the Monumental. One of them was in the Sarandi area of Buenos Aires, in 1906. By now a reasonably well-established club, River Plate decided for the first time in their history, to have their own stadium built.

When the day came for it to be officially checked out by a Football Association inspector, though, one big problem still remained – a total lack of a working water system. None of the pipework had been connected. All the club officials could hope was that the inspector would see the pipes and not bother to check any further.

They were out of luck. When he reached the changing rooms the inspector decided to test the showers. As he reached for a tap the officials showing him round turned away in embarrassment – only to turn back in amazement as a stream of water began gushing out! They were still reeling with shock when the satisfied inspector told them the ground had passed its inspection and left.

Had the water system suddenly been installed? Not quite. On the other side of the changing room wall two of the club's founders, Enrique Salvarezza and Alfredo Zanni, had set up some ramshackle piping leading to the back of the showers. When they'd heard the tap being turned on they'd pumped buckets of water into it and hoped the inspector was a bit of a drip!

THE BRICKLAYING MANAGERS AWARD...

Bob Paisley (Liverpool). Paisley was a Liverpool player who became a brilliantly successful Liverpool manager (1974–83), leading his team to 13 major trophies. Before turning professional, though, Paisley had been a bricklayer by trade. When he joined Liverpool in 1939 one of his first jobs was to help build the Anfield brick dug-out where he'd later sit as manager.

Playing with style

Clever thinking goes down just as well at village football level. After their pitch was dug up by a herd of wild pigs in 2002, the footballers in the Dutch village of Putbroek came up with a stylish solution to ensure that it didn't happen again. They covered their pitch with ... human hair! According to a local farmer: "Pigs have a very well developed sense of smell. As soon as they catch a human smell they run away, never to return."

Stadium stumpers

Every top team needs a top stadium to play in; and every top stadium needs a name to remember. For instance, everybody knows that Manchester United play at Old Trafford. But what does the word "Trafford" mean?

a) Theatre with a dream.

b) Area known for cream.

c) Valley with a stream.

Here's a quiz about some other top stadiums. Match the name of the stadium with the correct explanation of what its name means.

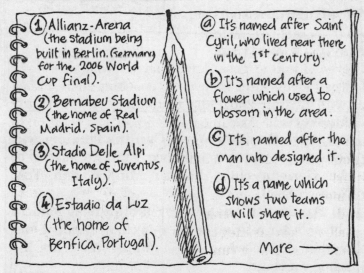

1. Allianz-Arena (the stadium being built in Berlin, Germany for the 2006 World Cup final).

2. Bernabeu Stadium (the home of Real Madrid, Spain).

3. Stadio Delle Alpi (the home of Juventus, Italy).

4. Estadio da Luz (the home of Benfica, Portugal).

a. It's named after Saint Cyril, who lived near there in the 1st century.

b. It's named after a flower which used to blossom in the area.

c. It's named after the man who designed it.

d. It's a name which shows two teams will share it.

More →

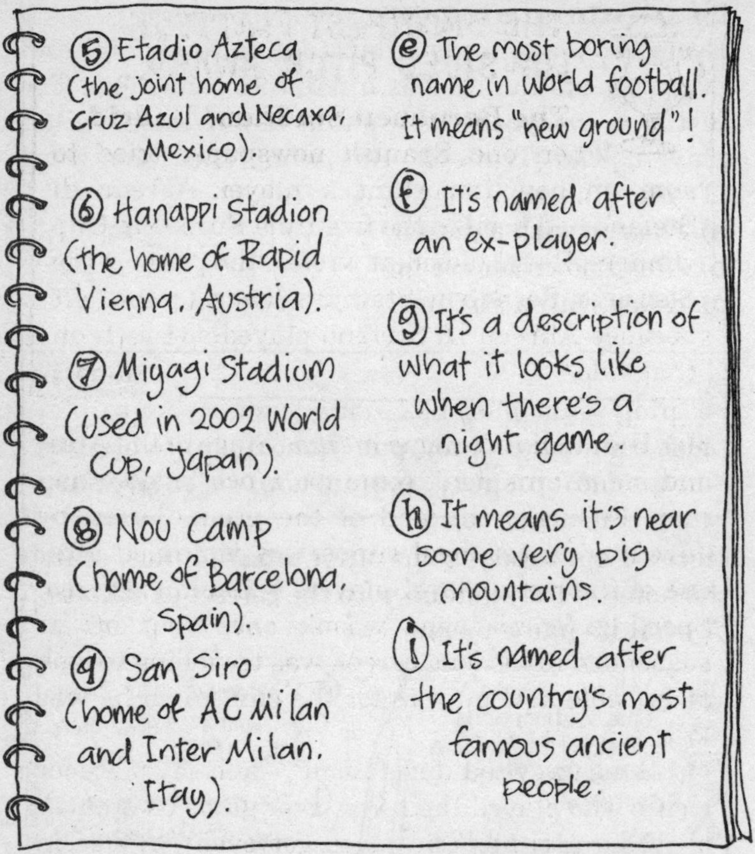

⑤ Etadio Azteca (the joint home of Cruz Azul and Necaxa, Mexico).

⑥ Hanappi Stadion (the home of Rapid Vienna, Austria).

⑦ Miyagi Stadium (used in 2002 World Cup, Japan).

⑧ Nou Camp (home of Barcelona, Spain).

⑨ San Siro (home of AC Milan and Inter Milan, Itay).

ⓔ The most boring name in world football. It means "new ground"!

ⓕ It's named after an ex-player.

ⓖ It's a description of what it looks like when there's a night game.

ⓗ It means it's near some very big mountains.

ⓘ It's named after the country's most famous ancient people.

Answers:

1d) After the 2006 World Cup the stadium will become the joint home (hence "alliance" arena) of the German clubs Bayern Munich and TSV Munich 1860.

2f) Santiago Bernabeu was a star Real Madrid player. After retiring he became club President and was in charge when the stadium that bears his name was built.

THE SMOOTHEST, FLATTEST, LOP-SIDED PITCH AWARD...

The Bernabeu Stadium, Madrid. When one Spanish newspaper tried to sum up how important a player Alfredo di Stefano had been to the five-time European Cup winners, Real Madrid, it wrote: "the pitch at the Santiago Bernabeu Stadium leans to the left because Alfredo Di Stefano played so much on that side."

3h) The stadium's name means "Stage of the Alps" and mountains don't come too much bigger than that! Fittingly, the end of the ground used by Juventus's most loyal supporters is named after one of their most loyal players – Gaetano Scirea. Sporting Scirea, who wasn't once sent off or suspended in his long career, was travelling to look at possible new players for the club when he was killed in a car crash.

4g) It means "Stadium of Light" – a flashy place for a club who played their first-ever game on a patch of waste ground! The place got even flashier in 2004. It was rebuilt in time for the European Championships in Portugal.

I'M OFF TO THE STADIUM OF LIGHT!

5i) The only stadium to host two World Cup finals (in 1970 and 1986), it's named after the native Mexican people, the Aztecs – who, fittingly, were famous for the beauty of their architecture. It's strong, too. In 1985 it survived a terrible earthquake in Mexico City, which destroyed over 800 buildings.

6c) Gerhard Hanappi wasn't just a top player with Austria's top club, he was also a fully qualified architect. So whereas most players just haunt stadiums when they retire, handy Hanappi was able to design a new one for Rapid. When he died, the stadium was named after him.

7b) The Miyagi stadium is named after the Miyagi area in which it's situated … and the area is named after the beautiful purplish-red or white miyagi bush clover blossoms, which flourish there every autumn.

8e) Needless to say, Barcelona moved there from their "old ground" in 1957. Before that they'd played in all sorts of dodgy spots, from a park to a place called Hotel Casanovas. Maybe that's why one of the first things they did was have the ground blessed by the Archbishop of Barcelona.

9a) Both the Milan teams, Inter and AC, now share the ground, although when opened in 1926 it was Inter's ground alone. The name San Siro comes from the area in which it's situated and it's still the name by which the stadium is known throughout the world. Officially, though, it's the Guiseppe Meazza stadium. Meazza played 408 games (and scored 287 goals) for Inter and was a World Cup winner with Italy in 1934 and 1938. When he died in 1979 the decision was taken to name the ground in his honour – although whether Joseph is a nicer name than Cyril is a matter of taste!

Derby ding-dongs

"Derby" matches are fans' favourites. What's so special about them? Well, funnily enough, it's nothing to do with how good the two teams are. Sometimes they're equally good, but they can just as well be equally bad. Neither does it matter if the teams are badly matched. One of them can be full of ball-balancing brilliance while the other is full of ball-battering badness. What matters in a Derby match is that it's between two teams whose grounds are very close together. This means that the fans live very close together, too – which means that the supporters of the winners will be able to taunt the fans of the losers every day of the week until the next Derby match comes around.

Two teams whose grounds couldn't get any closer are the Italian clubs Internazionale and AC Milan. That's because, as we've seen, they share the same ground – the San Siro Stadium. In 2003 it was the scene of the most peculiar victory ever seen in the European Champions Cup. Inter Milan and AC Milan had been drawn against each other in the semi-finals – so the first problem the two teams had to resolve was which of them was playing at "home" and which was playing "away" for each leg of the two-legged match. That's when it all got totally weird. With AC at "home", the first match was drawn 0–0. The second leg was also a draw, 1–1. But as AC Milan were now the "away" team, their goal was classed as an "away" goal and counted double. They went on to the final and won!

Derby games began in – come on, you should be able to guess by now – England! But in which English town was the first Derby match played?

a) Derby

b) Nottingham

c) Portsmouth

So why aren't Derby matches called "Nottingham" games? Because of yet another Englishman: a very posh one, the Earl of Derby. Not because he was a footballer, though; he wasn't. The enterprising Earl was a horse-racing fan and, way back in 1780, he founded just about the most famous horse race in the world: the Derby. (It's still being run – but not by the same horses, of course!) As the popularity of the race grew, so contests between near-neighbours began to be called "local Derbies".

Now every big football city or town has teams whose meetings are called "Derby matches" – and if you're looking for arguments and punch-ups, you won't find matches that are much worse. Compare the disputed score of that first Nottingham Derby with this collection and ask yourself: whose Derby games are foul, and whose are even fouler?

The Manchester Derby: Manchester United v Manchester City

The 1974 match between the two Manchester teams ended up with nobody left on the pitch! After a fight, referee Clive Thomas sent off both United's Lou Macari and City's Mike Doyle. When they refused to go, Thomas came up with a clever scheme – he took all the other players off the field instead! Macari and Doyle had no choice but to follow them. Crafty Clive then brought everybody beside Macari and Doyle back again to finish the match!

The Milan Derby: Internazionale v AC Milan

Inter fans have the one thing a supporter wants – a

taunt that can't be answered. In their case it's a chant of "Serie B" (B-league)! In 1979 AC Milan were found guilty of match-fixing and forcibly relegated. They bounced back up again but two years later were relegated once more, this time because they were hopeless. So why is it such an unanswerable taunt? Because, unlike their rivals, Inter have never been relegated.

The Buenos Aires Derby: Boca Juniors v River Plate

The teams who share Argentina's capital city have been rivals since River Plate moved away from the dockland area where both began to set up anew in a much smarter area. Since then, Boca Juniors have been known as the "workers' team" and River Plate the "snobs' team".

While the teams are battling it out, the fans like to call each other names. To bawling Boca fans, River Plate are "chickens" – that is, scared of them. It dates back to the 1980s when they probably were: at that time  Boca had the world star Diego Maradona in their team and won the Derby games every time! As for the roaring River Plate fans, their foul name for Boca is "pig". In fact, it's even fouler than that. The Spanish word for pigs is "bosteros", a word that comes from "bosta", meaning horse dung!

THE WETTEST RIVALRY AWARD...
Portsmouth and Southampton.

These two English teams meet in what they call the South Coast derby. Portsmouth proudly claim that they're the home of the Royal Navy. Southampton answer that they're the cruise ship capital of the world – to which Pompey fans like to reply, "Yeah – it's where the Titanic set sail from!"

The Glasgow Derby: Celtic v Rangers

The two Scottish clubs have a long history of both fabulous football and foul fights but on 17 October 1987 they were shown how to be even fouler – by two English internationals. Chris Woods, Rangers' goalkeeper, was sent off for punching Celtic's striker Frank McAvennie (who was also sent off for striking back!). He was followed by defender Terry Butcher, who put through his own goal, then followed up by trying to put Celtic's goalkeeper through *his* own goal.

Sherriff Archibald McKay, a Glasgow magistrate, showed that – unlike the players – he wasn't a fan of foul football. Butcher and Woods were both found guilty of a breach of the peace and fined.

IT WAS JUST ANOTHER DERBY!

The Montevideo Derby: Nacional v Penarol
But for foul Derby encounters, the Uruguayan teams Nacional and Penarol must be hard to beat. They were bad enough in 1990 when a massive fight broke out during their Derby game – and the referee set a record by dishing out red cards to 21 of the 22 players!

But in 2000, the sides hit an even fouler level. At the end of a bad-tempered 1–1 draw another brawl broke out. This time the police moved in with red cards of their own. Six punching Penarol players and three nasty Nacional men were arrested and thrown into jail for a week. They were only let out after promising to behave better in the future, and telling Uruguay's Ministry of Sport and Youth that they'd agree to give some free coaching to children.

126

So, have you made your mind up? Is football a fouler game today than it was when it first began to spread across the world?

Perhaps the answer is: sometimes.

What we all hope, though, is that football doesn't become even fouler as a result of players believing that winning is all that matters. It isn't. Football's a fantastic game, but that's all it is: a game about scoring more goals and having fun.

Let's end with the words of Alfredo di Stefano, who played in South America and Europe, and scored over 800 goals in stadiums around the world:

A soccer game without goals is like an afternoon without sunshine.

So have fun – and may the sun shine on all your football matches (especially at the other team's end!).

Foul Football

From the first mad matches with a pig's bladder to the cracking competions of the 21st Century, this glorious guide will give you the score.

Wicked World Cup

This international guide gives you the coolest commentary on the biggest, best, most talked-about tournament there is.

Phenomenal F.A. Cup

Following the highs and lows of the tournament, meet the giants and giant killers on the road to Wembley.

Triumphant Teams

From winning Wanderers to majestic Man U, meet the star squads from every decade of English football history.

Legendary Leagues

Discover top facts about champions of the English and Scottish leagues from the beginnings to the present day.

Furious Euro's

This goal-scoring guide tackles the pain and glory of the European Championships.

Prize Players

From Powerful Pete to Brilliant Beckham, this star guide features a winning line-up.

If you want to be in the game, get Foul Football!